YOU ARE NOT THE TARGET

A Message from Laura Huxley

Dear Reader:

Two of the Recipes for Living and Loving are not included in this book. Print would minimize their effectiveness, for they need voice and rhythm. Therefore, I recorded them. One of the recipes is called, "Your Favorite Flower." With this record we take a refreshing vacation from our everyday selves. While on this psychological holiday, many of us find, deep within, unsuspected splendors either forgotten or undiscovered.

In "Rainbow Walk" we take a walk together. We take it when you are ready to go to sleep: "You, who walk with me tonight, just feel and be—be what *you* are." We see a rainbow in the distance. By the time we blend with it, sleep takes over.

These two recorded recipes and the ones in this book are mutually independent. You do not need the record to derive benefit from the recipes you are reading, and vice versa. However, they complement and reinforce each other. They are good for each other—and for *you*.

With this conviction and my best wishes, I am cordially yours.

Laura Huxley

The cassette tape of "Rainbow Walk" and "Your Favorite Flower" is available from O.U.I., 6301 Sunset Blvd., Suite 103, Los Angeles, CA 90028 for $8.00. (Please, no cash, stamps, or C.O.D orders.)

YOU ARE NOT THE TARGET

*Transforming Negative Feelings
into Creative Action and Harmonious Relationships*

Laura Archera Huxley

FOREWORD BY ALDOUS HUXLEY

JEREMY P. TARCHER, INC.
Los Angeles
Distributed by St. Martin's Press
New York

Library of Congress Cataloging-in-Publication Data

Huxley, Laura Archera.
  You are not the target.

  Includes index.
  1. Happiness.   2. Large type books.   I. Title.
[BF575.H27H89   1986]   158'.1   86-1970
ISBN 0-87477-381-4 (lg. print)

Jeremy P. Tarcher, Inc.
9110 Sunset Blvd.
Los Angeles, CA 90069

Manufactured in the United States of America
10 9 8 7 6 5 4 3 2 1

First Edition

The author and publisher are not responsible for the consequences
of any individual or group therapy undertaken in persuance of the
theories, practices, or recipes outlined in this book. For permission
to teach the recipes, write to the author in care of J.P. Tarcher, Inc.,
9110 Sunset Blvd., #250, Los Angeles, California 90069.

ACKNOWLEDGMENT

My first thanks are to those people, friends, clients and students, who trusted me with their problems. Most of these Recipes are the result of the friendly cooperation of two persons intent on solving apparently insoluble problems. That trust and cooperation have been a heartening incentive to the writing of this book.

I am grateful to Virginia Pfeiffer, who years ago conducted me on a tour of self discovery which was an essential precondition to this present work; to her children Paula and Juan for their valuable reaction to my research projects and for the extravagant variety of new ones they present to me daily.

Since 1950, Professor Edmond Szekely and his wife Deborah have welcomed me and my projects at their unique Rancho La Puerta, at the California-Mexico border, and more recently at their Golden Door in Escondido. My gratitude to the Szekelys is only exceeded by my admiration for their work in the cause of good health and good human relationship.

I want to thank my editor, Ruth Goode, for her patience

with an inexperienced writer struggling to express ideas in a foreign idiom.

Thanks to Trude Shearman, who expressed her understanding and affection for this book by doing a wonderful job of setting and typing.

For reading the manuscript, for criticizing and encouraging, my warmest appreciation goes to Gerry Day, Joe Kearns, Christopher Isherwood and Gertrude Flynn.

Above all, it is to my husband that I owe my deepest thanks. At times, when intensely absorbed by a new idea, I would enthusiastically jot it down in an English that was not very English. His harshest criticism then would be, "Stop a minute—your English is getting just a little *too* eccentric!" There was never criticism without advice; there was always that extraordinary feeling of good will which is constantly present in him and of which, on this occasion, he gave with particular abundance.

LAURA HUXLEY

CONTENTS

FOREWORD
by Aldous Huxley

Human beings are multiple amphibians, living simultaneously in half a dozen radically dissimilar universes—the
molecular and the ethical, the physiological and the sym-
bolic, the world of incommunicably subjective experience
and the public worlds of language and culture, of social
organization and the sciences. Because they can talk and
think and pass on accumulated knowledge from one generation to the next, human beings are incomparably clev-
erer than the cleverest of animals. But because they often
talk foolishly, think illogically and reverence pseudo-
knowledge as though it were revealed truth, they can also
be incomparably more stupid, more unhappy, more cruel
and rapacious than the most mindlessly savage of dumb
beasts. Brutes are merely brutal; men and women are capable of being devils and lunatics. They are no less capable
of being fully human—even, occasionally, of being a bit
more than fully human, of being saints, heroes and geniuses.

Deliberate and consistent malevolence is rare. Most of
us mean well and would prefer, on the whole, to behave
decently. But alas, good intentions ineptly carried out are

the very things with which, proverbially, hell is paved. We can talk, we know the big words; nothing, therefore is easier for us than to enunciate a lofty ideal. The difficulties arise when we try to translate the ideal into practice. To achieve our noble ends, what are the means which must be employed? Precisely how do we intend to implement our high purposes? What must multiple amphibians do in order to make the best, for themselves and for other multiple amphibians, of all their strangely assorted worlds?

These are the questions to which, for the last two or three years, I have been trying to find answers plausible enough to take their place in a kind of Utopian and yet realistic phantasy about a society (alas, hypothetical) whose collective purpose is to help its members to actualize as many as possible of their desirable potentialities.* The writing of such a book requires a good deal of preliminary research—or, if that is too solemn a word, let us say a good deal of miscellaneous reading and the picking of a considerable variety of brains. Greek history, Polynesian anthropology, translations from Sanskrit and Chinese of Buddhist texts, scientific papers on pharmacology, neurophysiology, psychology and education, together with novels, poems, critical essays, travel books, political commentaries and conversations with all kinds of people, from philosophers to actresses, from patients in mental hospitals to tycoons in Rolls-Royces—everything went into the hopper and became grist for my Utopian mill. In a word, *je prends mon bien ou je le trouve,* I take my property where I find it—and sometimes it happens that I find it very close at hand. For example, I discovered that some of the clearest and most practical answers to certain of my questions were

* Now published under the title *Island.* Harper & Row, 1962.

being given by my wife in the "Recipes for Living and Loving," which she was composing for the benefit of those who came to her for psychological aid and counsel. Some of her recipes (for example, those for the Transformation of Energy) have found their way, almost unmodified, into my phantasy. Others have been changed and developed to suit the needs of my imaginary society and to fit into its peculiar culture. This literary debt is one which, along with all my other non-literary debts to the author of *You Are Not the Target,* I am happy to acknowledge.

One final word. Though my debt is literary, the material I have borrowed is more and other than mere literature. These recipes work. I have tried some of them on myself and have found them remarkably effective. And no wonder. Doing these recipes, I was forced to practice what, as a theorist of human nature, I had always preached —the great truth (so obvious once it has been recognized, but so constantly ignored even by those who ought to know better) that the life-problems of a multiple amphibian are many-faceted and, if they are to be solved, must be attacked simultaneously from many different angles.

The man of letters is tempted to live too exclusively in only a few of the universes to which, as a multiple amphibian, he has access. The schizophrenic is one who has completely succumbed to this temptation and who exists in a strange shadow world, a kind of homemade limbo. While lecturing at the Menninger Foundation in the spring of 1960, I was able, on a number of occasions, to meet with a group of far-out schizophrenics, who were receiving, every few days, an hour of music therapy. On several of these occasions I managed to induce all the members of this group to practice a version, somewhat modified to suit the peculiar circumstances, of the recipe "Your Favorite Flower." * The results were dramatic. With only one exception, these inhabitants of the shadowy other-world of mental illness returned, temporarily at least, to the substantial, human reality of here-and-now. A few minutes before, there had been no communication; now we could talk together. Questions were asked and answered. Personal anecdotes were recounted. Comments (often thoroughly sensible and to the point) were volunteered. The fact that men and women so extremely sick could respond in this way, albeit only for an hour or two, to one of these recipes was a remarkable tribute to the essential validity of what may be called the recipe-oriented approach. If far-out schizophrenics can get so much, how much more can the rest of us expect to receive? What can the recipe-oriented approach do for the mildly neurotic, the people with manageable problems, the healthy ones who would like to be still healthier and aspire to actualize yet more of their potentialities for love and intelligence and creativeness? There is only one way of finding out. "If *you* work, they work."

* This is a spoken Recipe, available on a 12″ L.P. record.

Part One

Part One

1. LOVE, NOT-LOVE

At one time or another the more fortunate among us make three startling discoveries.

> Discovery number one: Each one of us has, in varying degree, the power to make others feel better or worse.
> Discovery number two: Making others feel better is much more fun than making them feel worse.
> Discovery number three: Making *others* feel better generally makes *us* feel better.

There are almost as many ways of helping people to feel better as there are human beings. From among many recipes I have devised, here are a number which have proved exceptionally effective for a great variety of people.

Probably each of you will prefer certain recipes, and each will be stimulated by his experience to devise recipes of his own invention. It is the purpose of this book to quicken people toward realizing their creative potentialities *in their own way* in spite of all authorities, dogmas, tranquilizers, credit cards, and peace-of-mind-by-mail. Our creative potential has many aspects, but undoubtedly the most important one is to make good use of ourselves and what we are here and now, at each successive moment.

Total love has been recommended for centuries as the total panacea: obviously true, obviously unattained. Theoretically we all know that total love is the solution to all our problems, but in practice most of us behave most of the time as if this truth had never been discovered.

Whenever love is outweighed by not-love the organism is in trouble. Not-love may be brought about by the wrong inflection in a voice today, or by a nutritional shortage which began years ago. It may be the result of a sexual relationship with a companion whose chemistry does not blend with ours, or with one whose chemical affinity is harmonious with ours but whose mental and emotional being is inharmonious.

Not-love may be due to a loss in the stock market, to the non-arrival of an expected letter, to weariness and fatigue at the end of yet another day of dreary routine. Not-love may be the beaming smile with which a salesman must meet an important client, or a hostess an unwanted guest. It may stem from a serious loss or from some obscure endocrine reaction to climatic or atmospheric conditions. It may be due to too much of something or too little of something. Not-love may be the result of fanatical belief or secret doubt about the deity, church, party, ideology that we have chosen or have somehow been manipulated into choosing. Not-love may spring from a sound or a color, from a form or a smell. It may be a painful ingrown toenail or the release of the atomic bomb.

In all its manifestations and however it is produced, not-love tends to beget not-love. The energy of love is needed to reconvert not-love into love.

The essentials for *bare* living are food, water, and air.

What is the essential for *happy* living? We hear the answer
continuously:

> "I want to be loved.
> I want to love.
> I want to be loved.
> I want to love."

Disguised in a thousand forms, hidden under an infinite
variety of masks, love starvation is even more rampant than
food starvation. It invades all classes and all peoples. It
occurs in all climates, on every social and economic level.
It seems to occur in all forms of life. Love starvation wears
the stony face of the disciplinarian or speaks in the hys-
terical voice of the zealot. It puts on the unctuous manner
of the hypocrite or the ruthlessness of the ambitious power-
seeker.

Love starvation may camouflage itself in physical and
mental ills, in delinquency, sometimes death. In a family, love starvation begets love starvation in one generation
after another until a rebel in that family breaks the ma-
levolent chain. If you find yourself in such a family, BE
THAT REBEL!

Lately the value of love has been scientifically demonstrated. A group of scientists thought it useful to ascertain
the value of love and affection in the earliest stages of life.
For this purpose they took several newborn monkeys away
from their mothers and gave them mother substitutes in
the form of mechanical constructions. One of the constructions was made of wire and was the exclusive source of
milk: by pressing on a particular spot the infant monkeys
could get as much milk as they wished. The other substi-

tute "mother" gave no food but was made of soft warm cuddly material. The baby monkeys relinquished food almost completely, eating the absolute minimum to remain alive, and passed their time nestling against the imitation mother whose softness had some resemblance to a live monkey. The scientists decided that it is important for young monkeys to feel close to their mothers. This is love on the physiological level; as long as there is breath and the blood circulates, all love has a physiological aspect. Even the spiritual love for God has to be mediated through the body.

Working with dogs in his laboratory at the Veterans' Administration Hospital in Perryville, Maryland, Dr. W. H. Gantt has demonstrated the influence of affection on the functioning of the heart. "Some dogs, raised in the laboratory without enough human or canine companionship, become disturbed." In these animals, contact with man can be therapeutic. When a schizophrenic poodle was placed in the conditioning room his heart rate jumped to 160 beats per minute. As Dr. Gantt approached him, his heart slowed to a slightly subnormal 60 beats, and during petting to 20 beats per minute. "Even morphine failed to exert this strong an effect," Dr. Gantt observed.

Even a purely mechanical substitute for love can be of some value. It was found that newborn babies left alone in a virus-proof—and love-proof—nursery are quieter and happier, eat better and sleep better, when an artificial beat resembling that of the mother's heart is sounding in the room. How touching it is to think of these small creatures propelled into a cold, antiseptic world, longing for the animal warmth of the human skin, for human milk, a human smell and voice, being presented instead with electric blankets, reconstructed milk and an artificial heart-beat!

Yet, already in that first moment of independent life, and doubtless before, the chorus of born and unborn babies is singing in everlasting unison:

> "I want to be loved.
> I want to love.
> I want to be loved.
> I want to love."

The greater the urgency of this theme song, the more disastrous are the consequences of suffocating it. This cry for love is strangled and camouflaged by our own and other people's defenses, by our conventions and our taboos. "Love or perish," said Dr. Smiley Blanton, summing up in three words the past, present, and future of humanity.

What can be done to help a world desperately needing love and desperately afflicted with the infectious disease of not-love? Sociologists and educators, theologians, doctors and artists have offered prescriptions and suggested more or less elaborate treatments. But the problem concerns us all, not merely a few specialists. Moralists have proposed high ideals and issued categorical commands, but how are we to realize these ideals and obey these commands? We all want to be good and happy and to make others good and happy—but how? How?

The recipes in this book are designed for two purposes: to clear away the obstacles to the attainment of that goal, and to develop that part of ourselves that is longing to achieve that goal. Therefore the recipes are based on two fundamental principles: *the transformation of energy* and *the realization of creative potentials*.

But no recipes, no medicine, no prayers will be of any

use to us unless we have taken the most important step of all: the decision to produce a change inside ourselves. Not a change in my father or my mother, not a change in my wife, husband, children, not in anyone else—in myself. Let us initiate a change in ourselves, for then, and then only, shall we be able to effect a change in other people.

When we change, others change too. And circumstances change in a manner that is almost miraculous.

The initial change has to come from inside ourselves. If you have taken the momentous decision, then read on.

2. THE TRANSFORMATION OF ENERGY

"Energy is eternal delight."
WILLIAM BLAKE

We are alive because certain molecules have the power to transform the energy of sunlight into the raw material of life. If the lights come on when I press a switch, it is because the energies of falling water have been transformed into electric current. If the automobile moves when I step on the accelerator it is because the energy produced by the burning of fuel has been transformed from heat into mechanical action.

On all levels within the universe, animate and inanimate, the principle of transformation of energy is at work.

Human beings are the most prodigious transformers within the known universe.

We are physical transformers. On the physical level we transform air, water, and food into blood, bones, muscles, viscera, and nerves. To duplicate the work that our body does when we are, for instance, digesting our breakfast would take a superfactory manned by hundreds of skilled technicians operating the most stupendously complicated mechanical devices. And even then the duplication of digestion and assimilation would be incomplete—in fact, with our present technology, impossible.

We are intellectual transformers. What we see and hear, what we study and what influences us, impregnates our intellect and colors our thoughts and personality. We then transform all of this into ideas and actions according to our own nature and our particular needs.

We are emotional transformers. It is rare that we allow an emotion to remain in its raw state, particularly the emotions we are not proud of. Feelings that we have been brought up to regard as evil, such as envy, or hatred, are transformed into feelings that we have been brought up to regard as honorable, such as righteous indignation or moral disapproval.

The emotion of fear becomes converted unconsciously into timidity or resentment, the emotion resulting from injustice into either revenge or a sense of inferiority. The emotion of unrequited love or unfulfilled sexuality is often converted into prudery, irritability, or even cruelty. The emotion of guilt is often transformed into caution or, at the other extreme, into aggressiveness. Each individual transforms emotion according to his or her biochemical, physiological and psychological nature and in response to environmental and cultural pressures.

Next there is the deeply unconscious transformation of emotions into some kind of physical effects. Let us consider the mechanism of these transformations.

Emotions have power to change body chemistry, blood circulation, the output of hormones. What happens, for example, when a man feels the emotion of rage? His autonomic nervous system stimulates the adrenal glands. Adrenalin is poured into the blood and this stimulates the central nervous system, making him feel even angrier. At the same time the adrenalin in the blood causes the heart to beat faster and makes certain blood vessels contract, with the result that the blood pressure shoots up and there may be serious physical consequences.

It was an emotion which set off the chain reaction.

On the other hand, a tumor in one of the adrenal glands may lead a person to a permanent state of extreme irritability. This irritability is reinforced by the angry reactions of other people, and in response the glands are stimulated to pour out yet more adrenalin. The excess of adrenalin causes a further rise in blood pressure, again with the possibility of grave consequences.

In such cases, fortunately very rare, it is a physical disturbance that begins this chain reaction.

From these examples we can see how the endocrine system, the mind, and the body systems as a whole act upon one another in a circular way. The circle may be a vicious one, as in the cases just described. When the organism is functioning well, it is what we may call a virtuous circle. If there is a normal secretion of adrenalin a man stays alert and in a good mood, and if he is alert and in a good mood there is a normal secretion of adrenalin.

It may be because our emotions influence our whole being, that continually, and almost always unconsciously, we try to manipulate them in such a way that we may feel proud of them or at least not positively ashamed. But why should we be content to do this on the unconscious level? Would it not be better to transform the energy of our feelings in the full light of consciousness and in a constructive and liberating way? Most of us use our capacity to transform the energy generated by emotion in inappropriate and sometimes destructive ways.

But we do not have to do this. We have the capacity to

use our powers of transformation in the service of love and intelligence. This is a proposition with which, in a general way, everyone will agree. But general agreement is not enough.

We must apply the principle in practice, apply it to ourselves and apply it every moment of our lives.

The energy that activates our emotions is a neutral force. The energy that goes into behaving stupidly and unrealistically, that gives us the power to hurt others and destroy ourselves, is the same as the energy that goes into loving and being intelligent, that gives us the power to help ourselves and do a kindness to others.

It is *feeling* the energy, becoming conscious of it, that permits us to redirect it according to the best of our physical, intellectual, and ethical knowledge.

Our emotions and instincts have been with us much longer than our reason. Dr. A. T. W. Simeons' book, *Man's Presumptuous Brain,* is illuminating on this subject. He explains how the cortex, the seat of memory, association, perception and rational thought, has developed rather recently in comparison to the primitive brain which lies below the cortex and is the seat of our instinctive drives. These primitive instincts are as old as life. They generate emotions which are very powerful and are charged with an enormous amount of energy. If it is not properly used, this energy transforms itself into illness, physical or mental.

In many primitive societies this principle of transformation of energy is clearly understood and systematically acted upon. Rage, and the impulse to aggression brought on by frustration and anger, may be worked off harmlessly by violent action—yelling, dancing, stamping on the ground, hacking at a tree.

In our culture, we, too, get angry and feel frustrated, but our society generally does not approve of such overt expressions of our feelings. What would happen if a man or woman at a committee meeting or a PTA conference were suddenly to burst into a wild dance accompanied by yelling and stamping? Yet scientists tell us that fundamentally our instinctive reactions remain as they were before the development of our civilization.

Our emotions have their origin in primitive, often unrecognized instincts. These are very powerful, and charged with a vast amount of energy. If this energy is not acknowledged and beneficially used, it will find its own expression instead of ours. It will transform itself into irritability, or gastro-intestinal trouble. It will express itself in hidden hostility, or fatigue.

IMPROPERLY USED, ENERGY WILL RELEASE ITSELF NEGATIVELY THROUGH OUR PHYSICAL OR PSYCHOLOGICAL POINTS OF LEAST RESISTANCE.

The doctors can give us the physiological sequence of how these things happen. For the rest of us it is enough to know that they do happen—and that we can prevent them from happening.

Our task is to find ways in which the energy evoked by negative emotions can be transformed, in a manner compatible with civilized living, into harmless—or better—into positively useful energy.

Our purpose, then, is to become *expert and voluntary* energy transformers instead of involuntary energy victims.

Like everything else, this takes practice.

The basic recipe for practicing this is titled "The Art of Converting Energy." The Recipes "You are Not the Target," "The Tether Ball," "Be an Animal," "Bubble

Freedom" and some others are corollaries of the basic one. Begin with the one you wish to do. You need not begin with the basic one; choose the one that appeals to you most.

By your experience you will prove to yourself that both creative and destructive energies have the same source, and that it is possible to direct them. This will happen, not if you merely read and understand the recipes, but only if you carry them out. When you achieve this you will be able to direct your interior as well as your exterior life to a re- markable extent. When we become the intelligent direc- tors of this energy, then we can channel it constructively. Our capacity for transforming emotional energy can be used to our advantage in incidents and on occasions that arise many times during the day.

For this purpose it is necessary to keep in sharp focus a fact of which often we are not aware: we are at all times a connecting link, one of many links, in a chain reaction of related events. Each of us is the product of many chains: the evolutionary chain, the racial chain, the genetic chain, the environmental chain, and many others. The immense mass of events of which we are alternately the cause and the effect surpasses the human imagination.

Let us visualize all these chains as hundreds of millions of conducting wires, moving in space and time and con- verging on a single point. This point is each one of us, here and now.

Now, out of all these chains, let us consider for our pur- pose only one, the psychological chain. It is interwoven with all the others, but most obviously with the family, the educational, the cultural, the nutritional chains. By influ- encing the psychological chain we have gone a long way toward influencing our whole life.

To be able to choose how we wish to influence that chain, we must be aware of these two facts: that we are links in the chain, and that we have the power to change the nature of our own chain and consequently of those whose lives touch ours.

When we realize these two facts, we can do something here and now.

As an illustration let us imagine a small section of one of these chains. Let us say it is a chain of seven links, of which I am Number 7.

Scene: a suburb on the outskirts of a great city.
Time: early morning.

1. At the entrance of one of the houses stands a pot of fuschia in dazzling bloom. Mounted on a motorscooter a teenager comes roaring down the street, hurling folded newspapers at the front doors. One of his shots goes wide and strikes the fuschia a devastating blow. The shattered plant droops sideways, the flowers trailing in the dust. There are no witnesses to the disaster, and even the delivery boy is unaware of what he has done.

Thus is forged the first link in the chain—an accident, unintentional, innocent and therefore meaningless, or it should be. Let us see how it continues.

2. A few minutes pass. Then Mr. X, the owner of the house, comes out to pick up his paper.

What kind of man is he?

What will he feel when he sees what has happened to the flowers of which he was so proud?

How will he act?

Mr. X stoops for his paper and sees the broken flowers. His pride and joy, the result of months of tender care—all destroyed! Deliberately, he thinks, by that little devil. Filled with rage, he stamps back into the house. In answer to his wife's inquiring look, he launches into a violent diatribe against the whole race of boys—particularly that boy across the street. Mr. X is certain that the boy has purposely broken his flowers. "How do you know?" his wife asks. "Who else would it be?" Mr. X answers. And he goes on to say that Mr. Y, the boy's father, is always making trouble. The son looks exactly like his father—so who else *could* it be?

In this bitter, resentful mood Mr. X goes down the street to open his neighborhood drugstore.

3. Unfortunately, Mr. Y, the father of the suspected boy, goes in the drugstore to buy a cigar. Mr. X does not say anything about the fuschia, does not ask about the neighbor's boy. Had he asked he would have been informed that the boy had gone away to camp two days before. Instead Mr. X puts on his professional smile and congratulates himself on his self-control. But—cunningly—his repressed resentment finds a way to self-expression. Honest, precise Mr. X unconsciously shortchanges his customer.

4. Mr. Y, now at home again, opens his billfold to give his wife some money and realizes he has been shortchanged. At the disagreeable prospect of having to go back to the drugstore and confront Mr. X with the error, he is angry and indignant. He takes it out on his wife by complaining of her extravagance.

5. Mrs. Y goes out to shop. Among other items she stops to buy a brassière.

6. In the dressing room she is dissatisfied with her figure, and with the brassières she is trying on; underlying both annoyances is her memory of her husband's complaint

against the druggist, his unfairness to her, and a general anxiety on the whole subject of money. All of this adds up to a state of irritation, which she unthinkingly directs at the saleswoman who is unable to provide her with a satisfactory brassière.

7. I am the saleswoman.

At this point the negative chain reaction has touched me. It was initiated by a cheerful youth earning his pocket money by delivering papers in the early morning. It traveled from link to link, and now I am aware that a strong dissatisfaction, a powerful negative energy is being directed toward my person. My client's dissatisfaction may really be with her own figure, or the brassières, or anything in the world, but at this moment it is focused on me. What can I do about it?

I see four choices:

> I can pretend to ignore the unpleasantness. If I do this, certain muscular tensions and chemical changes take place in my body, changes of which I remain unconscious and which I have no power to direct. Psychologically, I am lying to myself.
> I can remonstrate with the woman and tell her to go and buy her brassière at some other store.
> I can be nice to my customer.
>
> OR I can acknowledge the impact of this negative energy and transform it to my advantage.

Let us see what happens in each instance.

> The first is a denial of reality which, if we make a habit of it, may have serious emotional and physical results and is one of the causes of psychosomatic illness. Besides, we cannot cope with reality if we deny it.
> The second may give me a moment of satisfaction but

it may have two bad consequences: one for my job and my business reputation, the other for the already disturbed woman.

If I really do not feel any animosity, if being "nice" does not make me a martyr in my own eyes, if my blood pressure does not rise and my muscles do not become tense—in other words, if I really understand the incident and am not hurt by it—then being nice benefits us both and it is indeed a good solution. But unfortunately it is a rare one.

Here is an occasion to apply the principle of transformation of energy. How?

I feel the impact of the negative energy.

I have trained myself to catch this energy, as though it were a ball.

I transform this energy and use it for a purpose I have chosen.

To be able to do this one must practice. This is the subject of the recipe "You Are Not the Target."

Our world is filled with free-floating energy, and we should become aware of the many ways in which we use it, both creatively and destructively.

A work of art is a clear example of energy used creatively. So is every human action or emotion that generates good in any direction, in any situation, in any degree. If you evoke a happy smile in a sad child, or if you build a magnificent dam, you are doing the same thing on a different scale: you are using energy creatively.

When we see someone shaken by pain, or trembling with rage, or overflowing with joy, we are readily aware of how much energy is encompassed in these emotions. The amount of energy compressed within the emotion of indecision is less obvious, but it is just as great.

You can demonstrate this to yourself with a simple test. Hold your two hands, palm to palm, a few inches in front of your face. Now, with all your strength, push your left hand against your right hand, and at the same time resist the push as hard as you can with your right hand and the entire right side of your body. Keep this civil war going for two or three minutes, pushing half of yourself against the other half: exhaustion is the result. This is what happens psychologically when you are in conflict with yourself and cannot decide which way to go. Your energy is spent in resisting one part of you with the other part. It is quite natural that so often you feel exhausted. Sometimes this pattern of self-resistance becomes a frozen chronic response to almost any decision. There are many other causes of exhaustion, but this is a common one.

War is the most terrifying example of energy directed against ourselves, and yet it was a great relief for many people throughout history. War provided them with a legitimate outlet for their aggressive feelings and an escape from their boredom. Even the humblest factory job acquired a glow of righteousness and patriotism. It is sadly significant that the number of suicides always declines during a war. A nuclear war would provide none of the satisfactions of past wars—no marching, no brass bands, no heroism. Like termites fumigated in their nests, we would all be exterminated, on any side of any curtain, by a stupendous gadget paid for by our hard-earned money and of which we were supposed to be proud.

This gadget is the most powerful of all man-made transformers of energy. My recipes are not quite so sensational as the H-bomb, but in their own way and on their own level they are effective for the person who puts them into practice. They offer the means whereby the enormous energies released in everyday life may be directed not towards dying badly but *towards living well.*

Part Two
Recipes for living and loving

The basis of RECIPES FOR LIVING AND LOVING
is PREFERENCE *for* LIFE

Man has no Body distinct from his Soul;
for that call'd Body is a portion of Soul
discern'd by the five senses, the chief
inlets of Soul in this age.

WILLIAM BLAKE

PROLOGUE TO THE RECIPES

As you begin these recipes imagine yourself to be a diamond. This diamond has many facets. Some of these facets are clear and limpid; some show a few specks of dust; some are covered with it; a few may be even mud-spattered. One opaque facet darkens all the others. One clear facet lets the light shine through all the others.

Each recipe that you experience completely will clear one or more facets of the diamond, and let more and more light shine through the others. The difference between being merely not dead and fully alive is the difference between being opaque and being translucent.

The recipes that follow are not for any specific kind of person or for any specific complaint. They are for anyone who wants to find harmony within the many sides of his personality, a balance within his physical and psychological being. They are for those persons who want to help themselves, not by suppressing any part of their being but by using everything in the service of the best of which they are capable.

The recipes frequently direct you to "remember" and at other times to "relive" or "re-experience" an episode of the past. Let us be quite clear about the difference between remembering and reliving.

Remembering is an intellectual function. With our memory we reconstruct facts, circumstances, people; we remember what we said, heard, or felt.

Reliving or re-experiencing a past event means exactly what the words say: we live, we experience that event again. Not only do we remember what was said; we actually hear it. We do not merely remember how people looked; we see them. If we were at a dinner we do not merely remember what we ate; we can actually taste it again. We do not remember that we felt elated; we are elated.

Some people naturally use their intellectual memory; others relive everything that they remember. Most of us use these two functions simultaneously although in different degrees.

When a recipe asks you to relive and re-experience rather than remember, do not be content with an intellectual reconstruction. Re-experience the event as fully as you can.

There are many directions in the recipes. These directions are not numbered or tabulated: this omission is deliberate. Numbers have different effects on people. Sometimes they are clarifying, sometimes confusing. So are other tabulations. However, the directions are so spaced as to give you ample place to put your own signs and tabulations. Maybe you prefer to use color signs rather than numbers—key words instead of letters of the alphabet— little mysterious symbols of your own instead of indelible printer's ink.

Read this book with pen and pencil. Put your own mark on it. Agree and disagree. Adapt and enlarge. Emphasize and remember with words, signs, colors. There is no one quite like YOU. *After a few months use, there will be no other book quite like* YOURS.

Do you have a pencil? Start NOW!

Many of the recipes ask you to stiffen or tense certain of your muscles. You may say: "That is just the trouble. I am already tense."

There is a fundamental difference between these two forms of tension.

When you tense or contract or stiffen a chosen part of your body voluntarily and consciously, you are directing the action and you are receiving benefit from it.

When you are involuntarily tense, you become the victim of misdirected energy of the nervous system and the consequent muscular response.

Another difference is that when we are involuntarily tense, we remain so, as though in a cast; but when we voluntarily tense a part of the body we also can voluntarily let go. Tensing and relaxing, inhaling and exhaling: these are the rhythms of life itself.

To divide body from mind is unrealistic and damaging. Body and mind are welded together throughout life. Let us use this oneness to our best advantage. One of the most important aspects of the Recipes is that they make us aware of this fundamental unity.

When carrying out the recipes, trace a response within your body to any emotion you may experience, unless otherwise advised. It is of value to trace and locate emotions in the body. Sometimes you are aware that an emotional or psychological experience has a counterpart in physical feeling. Sometimes it is difficult to recognize this. Then say to yourself, "If this emotion were to become a bodily feeling, let's imagine where it would be." Of this we will speak again in the recipes. The point is significant because it is by communicating with the feeling in the body that we liberate the energy encapsulated in that emotion and free it for our own conscious use.

Keep track of your reactions to the recipes. The best way to do this is to write a report to yourself after carrying out the recipe; note whether it was easy, difficult, mysterious, surprising, convincing, clarifying, etc. When you repeat a Recipe, note any differences in your successive reactions to it.

Before each recipe there is a page with blank space. Use it for your comments on the recipe itself. If you wish, think of the recipes as little plays in which you are the leading character. Keep track of the changes in that character, of his rebellions, doubts, fears, and progress—mark his victories. This is important, it concerns your life.

And please, give equal attention to the suggestion on the following page.

Let us beware of taking ourselves too seriously; we may become self-conscious dissectors of life, substituting recipes for living and loving in place of living and loving. Goethe pointed out this danger more than a century ago. He warned against the hypochondriacs of his time who were constantly and fruitlessly occupied with themselves. The real meaning of self-knowledge, he said, lay in taking notice of oneself in relation to other people and to the world.

In the recipes you are often asked to take a long, deep, slow breath. This is why: All other actions, thoughts, feelings stop while you direct your attention to breathing.

This kind of breathing brings about relaxation of the muscles, oxygenation of the blood, and clearer thinking.

Here is the suggested method for breathing in this way: Inhale through the nose—exhale through the mouth.

Exhale completely: make sure; there may be a little more air. Exhale any air left by sounding the letter ess.

When you feel completely empty, remain empty for a moment but not to the point of discomfort.

Then, very slowly, begin to let the air come into you.

Imagine that the air is coming in through the soles of your feet, up through your legs, calves, thighs. Let it come, slowly, smoothly in, through the sexual organs, through each vertebra of the spine, up through your neck, up to the top of your head. Imagine this air as energy, filling your whole body. Imagine, if you like, that the air becomes luminous when it comes into your body and slowly fills it. Keep the luminous air within you for a while. Now slowly let it flow out, not forcing it, and imagine that the air goes out carrying away with it any impurity of body or mind.

Refresh yourself by breathing this way from time to time during the day and on going to sleep.

These recipes contain directions. They ask you to do— then not to do. To experience the present—then, just as intensely, to relive the past. To be very active—then perfectly passive. All these seemingly incompatible directions have a single purpose—to make it possible for you to throw away all external directions and to direct yourself from within: to become what you really are.

"Which recipe shall I choose first?"

Consult the index, "Which Recipes for What Needs?" and the appendix, "Table of Personal Relationships," at the end of the book. However, I suggest you start with the following six recipes:

> You Are Not the Target
>
> The Tether Ball
>
> Jump Into the Other's Place
>
> Lay the Ghost, or Here and Now
>
> How Can I Use This?
>
> Dance Naked with Music

Here are a few hints about them.

"You Are Not the Target" is a recipe that practically all of us can use dozens of times a day. Whether most of our life is spent in work or in play, with the family or in groups, we can improve our psychological state and our physical assets. I cannot tell you how many people are using the recipe right now!

I suggest "The Tether Ball" because it is easy, and it has benefited every man, woman, or child who chose to do it.

In the last analysis most of our problems are problems of human relationship. "Jump Into the Other's Place" will improve your relations with others by giving you sharper discernment and understanding.

"Lay the Ghost" is effective when you wish to sharpen your attention and awareness. It is also used, when so in- dicated, as the last and essential step of some of the most important recipes.

"How Can I Use This?" will show you how to develop the habit and the ability of using even those feelings or facts which are or seem to be against you. It shows you that you can react creatively to destructive circumstances.

"Dance Naked with Music" may seem, to some readers, startlingly unconventional—yet I put it in this priority list because I have seen remarkable and even extraordinary results from it. If you ask, when you read it: "What is the point of this?"—*Dance,* and you will know what the point is.

1. *YOU ARE NOT THE TARGET*

or Use unpleasant emotions to make your body pleasing

When your husband complains—
When your wife nags—
When your boss is irritating—
When your friends are neglectful—
When your business partner is difficult—
When your child is unmanageable—

STOP!

Stop a moment.

Stop and realize that their irritability, irrationality, lack of consideration, coolness—in other words, their disagreeable and wounding behavior is not really aimed at you.

You may feel as though it were, but in the majority of cases it is not. You are *not* the target. You just happen *to be* there.

It is human sometimes to be irritable or unreasonable. It is also human for those of us within the radius of that explosion to feel that it is directed at us. Sometimes it is. Sometimes we are used as targets for the negative emotions of those closest to us. Most often, however, we are not the target. A husband, a wife, a child, an associate in business, even a stranger on a crowded bus may throw off a charge of anger or hostility which can be contained no longer, which must be discharged even at the risk of harming others.

This is a part of living, part of the interrelatedness of human beings. We cannot live in a world of people and avoid the storms of their disagreeable and painful emotions any more than we can avoid the weather. But we can avoid this feeling of being the target for them. We can even turn the unpleasant encounters to our own good use.

When a charge of negative emotion explodes in our direction, whether or not it is aimed at us specifically, we have an automatic response. The primitive self within us responds immediately and without our direction. It is part of our heritage of self-protective devices to rise to the challenge of violence or the threat of violence—even when it is no more aimed at us than a gust of wind or a wave in the sea.

Primitive people still respond to natural cataclysms in this manner. An eclipse is still seen as a warning of doom to mankind. An earthquake or a flood is considered as a punishment directed at a village, tribe, or nation for some offense against the unseen powers. Until three hundred years ago, if your cattle became sick it was because you were the target of a witch, and some unfortunate creature would be found and burned for it. If a man became impotent, a witch was believed to be the cause, particularly if the man was impotent only with his wife, but not with an attractive woman outside his home. In such cases, it was certain that he had been bewitched. This was deadly serious. In the sixteenth and seventeenth centuries, between half a million and one million women were burned alive—burned because people believed themselves to be the target of some imaginary magic power.

This kind of collective insanity is now over, but individually we still respond to another's negative emotions as though we were under personal attack. Although we would not consider ourselves the target of a hurricane or a tidal wave, we often feel we are the victims of meteorological disturbances in the minds of other people. Sometimes it is true; people are trying to hurt us. But most of the time they are merely exploding, and we happen to be nearby—a convenient substitute for their *real* target.

Whether or not the explosion is aimed directly at you, this recipe will enable you to use the experience for your own good.

Let us always remember that each one of us is part of an immense, probably infinite chain reaction. We have talked about this in Chapter 2. The nature of things is such that we are all links in an infinitely ramifying chain of reactions and events. The behavior of the worried, upset or unhappy person reacts on those around him, sometimes more destructively than an infectious disease. Most infectious diseases, such as measles or flu, are self-terminating after two or three weeks; whereas the neurosis, born of a bad experience, not only can last a lifetime, but can form a powerful and subtle chain reaction that goes on and on and is extremely difficult to stop. We can and often do pass on our negative responses to those who unwittingly come within our sphere, and they pass them on to others, ad infinitum.

For instance, if the head of an organization is a difficult and neurotic person, many men in his employ will become insecure and tense. Their state of mind, unless recognized and dealt with, will communicate itself to their wives who will react, in most cases, by becoming nervous, edgy or depressed; then the children feel the brunt of parental impatience and frustration and continue the cycle of resentful behavior toward their friends; these other children, in turn, will create difficulties for their parents and teachers who will let loose their disharmonious reaction on anyone unfortunate enough to be within range. And so it goes.

We use hygienic methods, vaccines and everything at our disposal to prevent ourselves and our children from becoming victims and carriers of infectious diseases such as typhoid, scarlet fever, polio, etc. It is our right and our duty to do this. It may not be as obvious or generally accepted, but it is also our right and our duty to protect ourselves and our children from the more subtle yet no less infectious and dangerous diseases spread by psychological contagion. We wouldn't think of going to a cholera-infested country without the protection of a vaccine. Yet almost every day we live and work in surroundings thickly infested with negative emotions—we literally plunge into them, often unaware and often unprepared. The contagion is, at times, instantaneous.

This recipe is designed to make us capable not only of avoiding infection but also of transforming the negative chain of disease-carrying emotions into something useful and beautiful.

Like the saleswoman in Chapter 2, each of us has a choice. We can passively take our place in the negative chain, accepting the harm to ourselves and passing it on to others. Or we can break the chain and turn the energy of a destructive emotion into a constructive action.

Energy is neutral. It is what we do with it that makes it destructive or creative, harmful or healing. The energy that we unlock from atoms can destroy all life on earth or it can make a better life on earth for all mankind. And we also know that energy is not itself destroyed, but only changed into another form.

A burst of hostile energy has its effect on you whether it is actually directed at you or whether you only think or feel that it is. Automatically, certain things happen in your body. Your heart beats faster; the rhythm of your breathing accelerates; your blood pressure rises. Tiny vessels open wider in your lungs so that more air enters and more oxygen is supplied to your blood. Even your liver receives a message to open its storehouse and release glucose—sugar fuel—into your blood. At the same time, the blood is hurried away from the digestive organs and, rich with oxygen and fuel, is rushed to the muscles.

This astonishing and complicated series of events is the body's emergency reaction. It is a survival mechanism that we share with our animal brothers. In the simple world of nature, this marvelous, instantaneous reaction takes place at the first sign of danger, preparing the body to fight or to run away. It saved our ancestors when they encountered a Stone Age cave bear or a mastodon; otherwise we would not be here today.

You are not likely to encounter a wild beast in the forest nowadays. But the lifesaving mechanism is part of you, and it goes into action whether you are facing a dangerous beast or a dangerous emotion. The same flood of rich and energizing blood rushes to your muscles, stimulating them to act, to move, to DO SOMETHING!

A bolt of hostile energy has been flung at you, and without your bidding your body has responded. Your muscles are ready and clamoring to act.

Under civilized circumstances, you are not likely either to fight or to run away. Yet your muscles are ready.

Then use them!

Use them to convert the unpleasant emotion into an action that strengthens and beautifies you.

That is the purpose of this recipe. But before we can use the energy of a distressing encounter for our own benefit, there are two things we must do.

First, we must realize, again and again, that usually *we are not the target*. It is our naturally egocentric nature that makes us feel we are.

And, equally important, we must *want* not to be the target. There is a widespread though subterranean feeling that to be made to suffer—to be a victim—is somehow an admirable position on earth and a good ticket to a special place in heaven. If we carry this belief in our subconscious mind, we will profit greatly from this recipe. It will help us to bring this subconscious wish out into the open where we can deal with it by converting it into free energy that can be used for our own good. If you know that you carry this belief in your own mind, ask yourself this question:

When do I do the most good for myself and for others:

> When I am suffering—
> Or when I am happy?

As this recipe is designed for dealing with unpleasant emotions that occur in the presence of others, it is obvious that we prefer to do nothing which is too noticeable. In a public situation our energy-transforming actions should involve only those parts of the body whose movements are not easily seen.

This is not as limiting as it seems. There are a great number of bodily movements that we can make without attracting notice. We can move or contract the muscles of our:

toes
ankles
calves
thighs
abdomen
buttocks
anus
genital organs
breast
chest
upper and lower arm
throat
tongue

You may find other muscles which you can contract and relax unobtrusively.

The essence of this recipe is the transformation of energy from a negative emotion into a specific muscular action.

The result is the perfecting of one or more specific parts of your body. We know today that muscular contractions strengthen and slim that part of the body as much as vigorous calisthenics. So before you begin to use this recipe, decide which part of your body you wish to strengthen or beautify.

If it is your thighs you have chosen, you can be confident that this exercise is as effective as any that exists for shaping and strengthening your legs and improving their circulation. If it is your abdomen, there will be a threefold benefit: you will restore good support to your internal organs and your torso; you will forestall intestinal disturbances and the mysterious lower back pains that haunt so many of us in our sedentary lives; and you will help your heart to keep your circulation going efficiently. At the same time, you lose inches off your waistline and gain in good carriage and good looks.

You can do either of these rewarding muscle contractions with no outward sign, standing or sitting. You will kill two birds with one stone: not only do you save yourself from the harmful effects of negative emotions, but you will also gain remarkable benefits in health and appearance.

Practice this for a few minutes:

Tighten the muscles of your thighs.
Pull them stiff, stiff, stiff.
Hold it—hold it as long as you can.
And let go.

Now, after you have done this several times, go back in your mind to a time when someone was irritating, insulting, unpleasant or unfair to you. But because there were others present or for other reasons, you could not, would not, or at any rate did not react openly. There are, of course, many reasons why we cannot always react openly to such a situation; it might mean losing a job we cannot afford to lose, or hurting someone we do not wish to hurt. The reasons are numerous, but the negative results are usually the SAME.

So go back. Relive that moment when someone, by a

word or a look or a silence, hurled a bolt of hostile energy at you.

And now—put this recipe into action: grasp that bolt of energy! Direct it with your mind! Thrust it into the muscles of your thighs—tighten—hold—and let go; tighten—hold—and let go; in rhythm—any rhythm you prefer. *Transform the energy of that destructive emotion into constructive muscular action* that will beautify and strengthen your legs.

To do this now, in retrospect, will give you relief from any feeling of hostility you may have carried in you since that unpleasant moment. But the particular value of this recipe is that it can be used at the time—on the spot— whether or not others are present. Practice it now in the privacy of your room so that you will be ready when you need it.

Tell yourself that you are NOT the target.

Decide which part of your body you wish to beautify and strengthen.

Contract and relax the muscles of the chosen part of your body in regular rhythms until you find the rhythm which is most comfortable for you.

Now, relive a moment of unpleasantness; and, as you feel the bolt of energy flying in your direction, immediately convert it into that rhythmical contraction and relaxation.

Now, you are ready to *live* this recipe, to apply it to new situations.

Be alert. Be ready for them. Your day, like everyone else's is full of opportunities to convert destructive energy into personal beauty and strength. The bus that fails to arrive on time, the gadget that will not work, the car that refuses to start—or the dear one, child or adult, who stretches your patience thin by thoughtless, irrational, sometimes deliberately provocative behavior—all the exasperating things and people that you must deal with during the course of an ordinary day may give you a full hour of this most effective exercise, without costing you a moment of valuable time. A person contracting the abdominal muscles ten times a day for ten seconds each time can lose between one and two inches from the waistline in a month. This is the principle of isotonic exercise which is now used by both the American and Soviet Olympic teams.

You can use this principle to great advantage on those occasions when you think or feel or know that you *are* the target. But whether or not you are the target, on such occasions you are the recipient of an energy that is negative *only if you accept it as such.* For paradoxically, when you transform negative energy by the contraction of a muscle, you use that energy to benefit the muscle, and therefore to benefit yourself.

This use of unpleasant emotions to make your body pleasant is one of the most important recipes in this collection—one that can be applied, again and again, throughout the day.

For instance, right now, is there any point in this recipe with which you do not agree? If so—fine. Go back to it. Read the paragraph in question again, and, as you disagree with it, contract the muscles of thighs or abdomen or whichever part of your body you have chosen to strengthen and beautify.

Read and disagree.

Contract and beautify.

As you read this entire book, apply this principle. If you read a passage which irritates you or with which you disagree, *take advantage of* your disagreement:

Read it again.

Read and disagree.

Contract and beautify.

Use this recipe for other areas of the body, continuously improving them. Its use brings us three great gifts:

It lifts us out of egocentricity by making us realize that we are not the actual target of all the unpleasantness we experience.

It fosters in us the practice of that difficult, but most rewarding art of living—the ability to transform something bad into something good.

It permits us to break a negative chain reaction, to transform a minus into a plus value.

When we are confronted by a disturbing emotional situation, unless we are able to behave in a *real* and not *imagined* Christ-like manner, three choices are open to us:

We can behave unpleasantly to others.

We can bottle up our feelings and so damage ourselves.

or—

We can transform the energy of destructive emotion into constructive muscular action, thereby improving our health, our appearance and our relationships with others. We can, out of bad will, create what is most needed—good will.

Which of these choices will you make?

It works—if you work

2. JUMP INTO THE OTHER'S PLACE

Some years ago, when I was living in Italy, I had a maid called Maria. She was as competent as she was charming, and we got along very well together. Maria was happy with her salary, a little higher than her usual pay, and I was delighted to have a helper so willing and able.

One day I was getting ready to go out and, as women so often do, I had misplaced my handbag. In a hurry, and a little irritated at myself, I called out, "Maria, where is my bag?"

Maria appeared, white as a sheet. "I didn't touch it, Signora. I didn't touch it! You think I am a thief. I go. I will take my things and go home at once. I do not care about your money!" And, half in rage, half in tears, deeply hurt by what she believed was an accusation, she began to take off the pretty uniform she had been so happy to wear.

Some years later, in a plush Beverly Hills dental office, a dentist of good standing was preparing to file a tooth which we both had agreed it was advisable to cap. Out of mixed scientific interest and personal concern, I asked, "Will this treatment weaken the tooth?"

At this the dentist straightened, looked me in the eye, and exclaimed, "You do not trust me! You have no faith in my skill! Why should you ask such a question, implying that I am going to ruin your tooth? Why do you want to offend me?"

Different as they were on the surface, in essence these two incidents were alike. In both, I was concerned about myself and asking for help: from Maria, help in finding my handbag; from the dentist, the psychological help of explanation and reassurance given by the expert who was about to work on me. Yet both felt themselves accused, both were deeply offended. How could my appeals for help have been so misinterpreted?

Yet, seeing the situation with *their* eyes, hearing it with *their* ears, it is not hard to understand.

Maria heard the annoyance in my voice—annoyance at myself, but how could she know that?—coupled with a demand for my handbag, my money. To a girl reared in poverty, money was of utmost importance. More important still was her reputation for honesty, her good character, without which she could not find work. Perhaps the little maid had been tempted at one time or another; perhaps, at the price of a hard struggle, she had resisted the temptation to touch an employer's money. How sensitive this nerve was! Only those who have known poverty and worked for others better off than themselves can imagine her feeling. Unknowingly, unthinkingly, I had touched this sensitive nerve.

And the dentist. For reasons of his own, he, too, was sensitive on the subject of his professional skill and judgment. Perhaps it had been repeatedly questioned by a person important in his life; perhaps the competition was severe. Who knows what his inner doubts may have been? To him, the concern expressed in my question—concern only for my tooth—was a thrust at his self-confidence and a prod to his self-doubts.

Could I possibly have foreseen the reactions of my sensitive little Italian maid and of my touchy American dentist? But one could also ask: why should I *not* have foreseen their reactions?

All of my afterthoughts about these incidents, which explained the misunderstandings to myself, could have been thought out in advance. I could have predicted that Maria was likely to be sensitive about her honesty—that the dentist might be no less sensitive about his professional standing. Yet I had offended them by the manner and tone of my appeals. In both instances, I had been concerned so exclusively with my own interests that I had failed to take account of theirs. And I had been startled and shocked by their excessive emotional responses.

All of us have been startled by similar responses when we least expected them. Sometimes we are the offenders, sometimes the offended. Often, in sheer self-defense against the other's attack, we react with equal inconsiderateness and violence. A chain of misunderstanding is begun, a chain of hostile and painful reactions, a chain of thrust and counter-thrust, of wound and reprisal.

How can this person be so completely unreasonable, incomprehensible and illogical? How shall I deal with him—for deal with him I must—when his reactions are so strange to me that I, in turn, am astonished and offended, enraged and humiliated?

Every individual has his own way of responding. Some of us try to placate; some strike back. Some give a logical answer; others only talk louder and longer, trying to drown out the offended one's protest. Still others plunge into an ever blacker, heavier silence. If they are close and important to each other, two people locked in such a chain of responses can make themselves and each other physically ill—and never know why.

Quarreling—to give it its everyday name—can be salutary. It can lead to better and clearer understandings, to warmer and kinder feelings. But it can do this only if *victory ceases to be the object*. It can do this only if one or the other, at some point, puts down his weapons and tries to see the situation with the other's eyes—to hear it with the other's ears—to jump into the other's place!

Quarrels are as infinitely varied as human relationships themselves. No one can make a general rule about them.

But in every encounter, we benefit ourselves and the other if we cultivate the art of being able to *jump into the other's place*.

To learn this art is the purpose of this recipe. Here are the directions:

> *Choose a moment when you feel fairly well and have a certain measure of control over your emotions.*
>
> *Isolate yourself in a quiet place.*
>
> *Get comfortable. Lean back. Close your eyes.*
>
> *Recall a specific incident involving a person with whom you often quarrel or have friction of some kind.*
>
> *Begin to see and feel that specific situation.*
>
> *Hear the beginning of that dialogue.*
>
> *Feel the temperature.*

See those surroundings.

Go through the incident once from beginning to end.

And now, instead of trying to understand the other person, drop this effort completely.

And, with a bounce of the imagination, jump into the other person's place.

Now, go through the same incident from the beginning; see the same people and hear the same dialogue—but this time from inside that other person.

In order to do this you must, for the moment, put yourself aside. Withdraw all energy from your thoughts and emotions and use that energy to jump into the other's place. This is not easy but it is of great value. Many books have been written about it. Read them another day. Today, just do it. Quietly, determinedly and surely, take the whole of yourself, good and bad feelings, thoughts, ideas, sensations, and put them away somewhere—just for a while. There is no danger of losing them. They are not easy to lose.

Jumping into the other's place can be done, just like that, by a leap of imagination. For many of us that is the natural way; for others, here is another, slower way which may be easier:

Imagine yourself sitting or standing or walking just as the other person is doing.

Imagine your face expressing what his face expresses, your hands moving just as his move.

Now you are the other.

You feel as he feels.

You think as he thinks.

You see you, hear your voice and your words, as he does.

You feel frightened, threatened, bored or disgusted, as he does.

Feel your heart beating like his.

Now again, go through the incident.
You are the other person.
You respond as he responds.
And you see yourself as he sees you.
Little by little, you become the other. You enter inside the other.

Feel the blood pressure.

Feel the tension of his muscles.

Feel the reaction of his body.

Feel the great universe inside the other, think his thoughts, feel his emotions.

Last come his words, the final awkward outcome of an immense and mysterious chain of events.

Feel those words from inside the other person, the way he feels them, the way they really are for him, the way they feel in his body before and while and after they are spoken.

Wordy or silent, quiet or violent, feel this entire incident from inside the other person.

It is one thing to accomplish this in solitude and privacy. It is another thing to jump into the other's place in the heat of an argument or quarrel. But the exercise will help. Even if we can enter into the other's world just a little, how much more intelligently we can deal with him—how much less wounded or disturbed we will be by his actions and words. And we will make a surprising discovery: when we understand *others* better, they like *us* better.

Three thousand years ago the god Siva said to his wife, the goddess Parvati: "Feel the consciousness of each person as your own consciousness. So, leaving aside concern for self, *become each being.*"

It works—if you work

3. THE TETHER BALL

A tether ball can be bought for about five dollars in a sports store. Sometimes it is sold with a long pole, and in this form it is often seen in schools. For our purpose, we do not need the pole.

Hang this ball on a nail at about the height of your nose.

Punch it.

As you punch, think of that irritating person who thinks he knows more than you do, and whose mistakes you have to correct all the time.

Punch harder.

Feel how unjustly you were treated as a child, how often you were punished for offenses of which, in your own mind, you were wholly innocent.

Punch *harder*.

Think of whatever or whoever irritates you today—your parents, your children, your husband, your wife.

Punch—punch—punch.

Punch your irritation out.

Punch out their lack of delicacy, of awareness, of love.

Punch.

Punch. Even if the ball no longer seems a ball, but takes on another aspect—keep punching.

Punch—with fear or rage.

Punch—with despair or resentment.

Punch out all these feelings. The more you punch, the less will be the power of these destructive feelings to hurt others or yourself. So long as they remain pent up inside of you, they can do harm. Punch them out—punch them into a ball whose function it is to be punched.

If you happen to be that one person out of a million who has never been hurt, and who has never felt hurt—if you are that one in a million who has completely forgiven himself and everyone else, who has accepted and understood the merciless cruelty of sickness and war, of children dying of hunger, and old people of loneliness—if you are this rare creature then you are very fortunate and have no need for this particular recipe.

You may think the tether ball is too simple a device to relieve your complicated, unique, often obscure emotions; sometimes it is. But do not make up your mind in advance. You cannot judge the tether ball's value until you have used it for three or four weeks.

Almost every human situation arouses mixed and complex feelings. Often these feelings have their roots in events that took place in the distant past. Whatever their origins and complexity, whatever their separate and individual effects, they all affect the body as well as the mind.

In many cases there is overstimulation of the glandular system with the result that toxic amounts of adrenalin are poured into the blood stream. Adrenalin is a powerful stimulant. An increase of the amount of adrenalin in the blood brings about changes in the functioning of the organism. Those changes are ordinarily associated with an increase in muscular and nervous tension. *If the tensions are not discharged,* they arouse unpleasant feelings, undesirable changes of mood, even physical pain and illness.

This is why the simple honest tether ball is of such value.

When you punch it with full awareness of the feelings that you are discharging, you are liberating yourself *through consciously directed muscular activity* from the negative emotions that cannot otherwise be discharged without harm to yourself or others.

These deep-rooted, powerful feelings cannot be exorcised by verbal formulas. Often, they have been brought on by words, your own or others', but now they have been translated into bodily changes. These word-produced feelings are incorporated into your physical self, your complex bodily mechanisms. These words are no longer mere words: They have become driving impulses communicated along nerve and muscle fibers. They cannot be *talked away.*

But they can be *punched away.*

One of the most direct, most honest ways to deal with these negative emotions is to recognize them and give them harmless expression through physical action.

In this way *we do not deny the unpleasant emotions. We transform them* and their bodily consequences.

To be able to create something good out of something bad—this is the art of living.

Negative emotions, such as irritation and anger, are psychological toxins. Their poison does not merely infect the mood, the state of mind. It runs through the body, runs in the bloodstream to every nerve and muscle. Fortunately it is within our power to rid ourselves of the psychological poison, and so open the way to the free flow of affection and love.

Few methods do this as quickly and effectively, as freely directed punches and kicks—freely directed, remember, at a ball which does not suffer, whose function is to be punched and kicked.

Do not look down on the tether ball, for it has brought relief to very intelligent and gentle people. It has been healthful for a poet and for a minister. It has been used to great advantage by frail young beauties and by benevolent elderly ladies.

This ball is very useful to men and women in executive positions. I know of an outstanding businessman who has a tether ball under his desk, one in his car, one in his bathroom, and he takes one in a suitcase whenever he goes on a trip. Since he has done this, his large organization is running more smoothly and efficiently; his blood pressure does not bother him, nor does his girl Friday get on his nerves. Of course he doesn't know that his girl Friday has one tether ball under her desk, one in her car, one in her apartment. . . .

Within families, the tether ball has helped to turn many destructive moments into unifying ones. It has opened channels of good feeling in the minds of accusing or self-condemning wives, of restless, embittered husbands. I have found it most revealing to note that when a wife comes home with a new tether ball, which is, after all, a rather unusual purchase, her husband scarcely shows surprise. Instead he joyfully falls to. And both feel better for it. It has liberated parents to deal wisely with their children, and children to accept wisdom from their parents.

The tether ball is a simple, safe, direct-action antidote to toxic feelings. There are several ways to use it. Each time you use it, do it with the *conscious awareness that you are ridding yourself of negative emotions:*

> Suspend it from the ceiling, or from a hook on the wall, and punch it. Punch out what has made you angry. Punch disappointment and frustration out of your system.
>
> Fasten a long rope to it and kick it. Pull it back and kick it again. Know what it is you are kicking.
>
> Take it between your hands and squeeze it. Squeeze out of it the feeling that bothers you. (This use of the ball, incidentally, is a very good exercise for lifting and firming the breasts.)
>
> Find new personal ways to use it. Let your imagination lead you. For example, here is a special hint for victims of the telephone: take a medium-size ball and put it between your knees. Every time the conversation takes an exasperating turn, give the ball a tight squeeze— and another—and another. Result: better mood and firmer muscles.

Important: Before going out for a drive save just three minutes for the tether ball. Thousands of accidents are caused by tension, irritation, or anger. Our way of driving reveals much of our feelings. These three minutes may keep you out of trouble with the police, or even save you from an accident.

> Remember all the inept and discourteous drivers you have seen on the road.
>
> And punch the ball.
>
> Remember the policeman who stopped you when you did not think you had done anything wrong.

Punch.

Think of the fine you had to pay.

And punch.

Having freed yourself from the tensions and irritations associated with driving, go out and enjoy your drive!

It works—if you work

4. *LAY THE GHOST*

or HERE AND NOW

This recipe may seem to you strange, even eccentric. Yet its principle has always been known to mystics, philosophers, educators, and psychiatrists.

It takes just ten minutes.

It has two uses:

> *It is to be done at any time when you wish to sharpen your attention and awareness.*
>
> *It is to be done, when so indicated, as the last and essential step after some of the more powerful recipes.*

The first use is immediate and practical and you will quickly grasp its value. That is, to sharpen your attention and awareness, to bring your entire being, your psychological and physical self into focus, making *all* of you alive and functioning together now, at this present moment.

Often a part of us, of our attention, of our energy, is trapped in the past and we are not even conscious of it. Our memory is a complex mechanism. We have many kinds of memory. For our purpose here we will talk about the two principle kinds: the information memory and the emotional memory. They are not neatly separated. Our information memory is indispensable to our normal living; without it we would not know how to read and write, how to perform any of the learned skills that implement the process of thinking. When someone possesses this kind of information memory to a phenomenal degree we say he has an encyclopedic memory.

The other is our emotional memory. It is the memory of emotions connected with events, people, and places. At times the emotional memory pervades our whole being. I recount to a friend something funny that happened to me. I laugh. I am shaken with laughter. I am recalling the facts of a past event, but as I do so my mood changes and my body chemistry changes from what it was when I began my story to a state of convulsed amusement. It is not the information memory of the event that produces those changes; it is the emotional memory that does it.

The emotional memory is also charged with negative emotions. The emotions of long-forgotten unhappy events can invade our present in a subtle, indefinable way.

The unconscious emotional memory can take our energy and attention and interfere with our living in the here and now. Without our knowledge the memory of the past often makes us react today as we reacted long ago. To illustrate:

Let us imagine two men taking a walk in the country. It is a lovely day, with white cumulus clouds heaped on the horizon. The first man points out how luminous the clouds are in the sun. But the other feels a pang of anxiety—those clouds may presage a sudden storm. His pleasure is spoiled, not by the harmless clouds of this fine day, but by a cloud of the past, a storm that burst suddenly, perhaps twenty years ago, when he was a small boy. Probably the fright of an adult, rather than the storm itself, frightened him then. Now he is a grown man, and the sight of potential thunderclouds even in the sunshine worries him. In his unconscious emotional memory the ghost of that childhood storm still lives and distracts him from the pleasure of his present-day walk in the country.

All of us have experienced a ghost memory that rises up unaccountably and makes us uneasy and inattentive, unable to function fully in the present. At such times, in the few minutes that it takes to do this recipe we can disperse the beclouding memory even if we cannot identify its source, and give our full attention to here and now.

The second use of this recipe, is as a follow-up, when so indicated, after certain other recipes.

The practice of some of those recipes takes you into moments of the past, with the purpose of finding and liberating the energy that was imprisoned there. By practicing "Lay the Ghost" as a final step, you complete the process. You bring that liberated energy back with you to the present, to this moment of living.

That is why it is of first importance to do this recipe at the end of others when it is indicated. Indeed, it is better not to begin one of those other recipes at all if you do not save ten minutes at the end for "Lay the Ghost."

Here are the directions:

> *If you are sitting or lying down, get up and move around.*

Now:

> *Blink your eyelids twelve times, very lightly and quickly, as a humming bird flutters his wings.*

Stretch your arms wide towards the horizon. Stretch wider and wider.

Blink as before, fifteen times.

Now stretch towards the sky, higher and higher.

Yawn enormously—like a hippopotamus. Yawn as long, as wide, as many times as you can.

Blink as before, twenty times.

Feel your feet touching the floor, or shoes, or stockings, or whatever touches your feet.

Swallow three times.

Notice four objects in the room.

Drink a glass of water.

Count ten hairs on your head—pull out three.

Touch five objects in the room.

Let water flow on your wrists for a few seconds: cool if you are hot, hot if you are cool.

Open the window and breathe fresh air.

Make yourself sneeze (directions below).

Freshen up your clothes and face.

Say your name, the day of the week and the date, aloud.

Look at, touch, smell something you like.

Throw something up in the air and catch it; do this ten times.

Check your appointments or plans for the rest of the day.

> Give a quick thought to the most pleasant thing that is going to happen today or tomorrow.
>
> Say your name, the day of the week and the date, aloud.
>
> Check the time of day.

As you see, the acts are grouped in three sections, but only to make it easier for you to memorize them. They are to be done in swift sequence, as quickly as possible without stopping between one and the next. Perhaps you remember or have seen in a revival one of those early silent films, a Chaplin or Mack Sennet comedy, in which everything moves at a breakneck pace. When you have learned and practiced this sequence a few times, go through it at a similar pace, not pausing, not thinking, simply doing.

If you have a questioning turn of mind, you will see why. These acts are totally unrelated to each other. Each one uses another set of muscles, nerves, senses. Each one demands concentration on itself as you do it. When you blink, and count the number of times, you are aware only of your eyes and the eyelids swiftly closing and opening over them. When you count ten hairs, the touch senses of your fingertips have your whole conscious attention, and when you pull three, you feel the three separate, sharp little jerks in your scalp. Every one of these steps has its purpose and its value, including the sneeze.

Here are the directions for sneezing:

> Take the corner of a facial tissue and roll it with your fingers until it is two or three inches long. Insert it gently in first one nostril, then in the other, until you find a place that is particularly ticklish. Tickle that place until this stimulation brings about a sneeze.

Be sure to use this recipe in conjunction with the others, to free your energy and attention from your excursion into the past.

Be sure to use it by itself, at those times when you feel the need to pull together all your powers to deal with, or to enjoy fully, your life here and now.

I would like to tell you how "Lay the Ghost" got its title.

Several years ago when I was in Florence for a few weeks a priest asked me to see a young girl in his parish. He said she had a feeling of persecution, and perhaps I could do something for her.

Luigina was a sweet, studious girl of seventeen. She said that she felt all right except for *"l'omino verde"*—the "little green man."

"The little green man? He sounds interesting. Who is he?" I asked.

"That is just the point," Luigina said, "I don't know whether he is real, or a dream, or my imagination, or a ghost. For years he has been around, and I am getting more and more afraid. Please tell me—you must know— is he real or a dream or a ghost?"

"I cannot tell you, but soon you will be able to tell *me*."

The incident had happened nine years before. Luigina, then eight years old, had a dream—but was it a dream? It was so vivid that she never could decide whether it was a dream or a real fact. The "dream" was simply that a short man holding a green lantern, which made him look green, had come near her bed. This was in the country and there were no lights in the house. She had awakened, frightened, and had run to her parents' room screaming that she had seen a little green man. Instead of listening to her quietly, her parents had made fun of Luigina for seeing ghosts, and for a long time afterward they would sing "Luigina sees a little green man."

The scorn of the grownups, the reality of the dream, the deadly mixture of fear and ridicule had accumulated through the years, and Luigina, although seventeen, was underneath a frightened and confused little girl of eight. She could not remember her lessons—she thought she could not even marry if she did not know whether the little green man was real or a dream or a ghost. The family had long since ceased talking about him, but the damage had been done. Luigina could talk about her strange fear only to the priest, her confessor, who had sent her to me.

With a little coaxing she went back more and more real-istically into the incident; she relived it, and the emotion and the fear in it were terrifying. A little eight-year-old girl, alone in the darkest night, dreams or sees an un-friendly man with a green lantern coming nearer and nearer her bed—and when she finally can run away from him she finds only mocking laughter from those to whom she goes for help.

After she relived the event with me a few times, we did "Lay the Ghost" together. At first she thought it strange, but she followed my directions. Then I asked her to go back to the frightening incident and look at the little green man again. She did—and was surprised to find very little reason to fear him.

Then again we did "Lay the Ghost," very fast this time, for she knew the routine. She began to have some fun with it. Again I asked her to go back to look at the little green man. This time when she looked at him a rather amused expression came over her face.

Again we went through "Lay the Ghost," this time at

lightning speed. As we were doing it I saw surging through her the deepest, most marvelous laughter; every cell seemed bathed in it. "Now, tell me, Luigina," I asked, "is the little green man real, or a dream, or a ghost?"

She could hardly answer, the laughter was so wonderfully invading.

"What do I care what he was," she finally brought out. "From now on I am going to make a mascot of him!"

"Thank heavens," I thought to myself, "we laid the ghost."

Big or small, frightful or absurd, most of us carry around our quota of ghosts. Over and over, we come upon the frightened or angry or frustrated children we once were, and the child may terrify or paralyze the adult. Wise men have always admonished us that it is necessary to learn to live here and now. When Christ said, "Let the dead bury the dead," and "Sufficient unto the day is the evil thereof," He was telling us to put away the pains and mistakes of the past, and live here and now.

These ghosts of the past have two common characteristics:

They are energized by a past fear.

They are parasites. They deplete our energy and capacity for coping with the present when it is difficult and enjoying it when it is enjoyable.

So let us lay those ghosts, once and for all, HERE AND NOW.

It works—if you work

5. HOW CAN I USE THIS?

Even for the luckiest of us life is not always happy. At one time or another everyone has to face the shocking facts of injustice and frustration, of sickness, despair and bereavement.

We cannot guarantee ourselves against misfortune; but we can do something to transform the evils that afflict us into a less painful, even a creative reality. We can do this by asking ourselves the question:

HOW CAN I USE THIS?

"This" can be anything that is in the process of using us. It can be anything from an annoyance to a catastrophe, from a twinge of disgust to an access of desperation. I have become the victim of *"this."* How can I turn the tables? Instead of being misused by *"this,"* how can I make use of it?

It is when we are physically well and mentally alert that we must implant the question deep within ourselves. Each of us can word it differently, but its meaning is: "How can I use this distress, this pain of mind and body which is *misusing* me?"

It is necessary to catch ourselves at the first onset of *"this"* whether it comes suddenly as a shock, or in an insidious subterranean way.

When we are hurt, either physically or mentally, our awareness diminishes immediately. As a sponge absorbs water, so do physical pain and mental distress absorb our awareness. From acute awareness to complete unconsciousness there is a continuum of many degrees. In a single day we go up and down the scale of awareness—from a confused apprehension of what is going on around us to a sharp perception of outer events and inner feelings.

If we implant our question at times of keen awareness it will ask itself automatically at the needed moment— that is, at the onset of *"this"* when probably our awareness is lowered. There is a paradox here, for we have to remind ourselves of the question at precisely those times when it is not necessary for us to ask it. ". . . tasks in hours of insight will'd / Can be through hours of gloom fulfill'd" was Matthew Arnold's way of saying it.

Outstanding people are outstanding because, among other reasons, they know how to use bad circumstances in a creative way. Nehru used his term in jail to write his best book. Helen Keller used her inconceivably limiting handicaps to demonstrate the infinite potentials of human beings and to give courage to people apparently much better off than herself. Good writers use whatever happens to them, whether good or bad, for their books.

Dr. Arnold A. Hutschnecker, in his book *The Will to Live,* tells us that even illness has its positive uses. In his long experience with people suffering and in pain, this physician saw many who emerged from illness more mature and capable in the art of living.

Recently I saw a mother skillfully turn to advantage the injury to her son's knee. The child was screaming more at the sight of blood than from pain. He kept repeating "Blood! Blood! Blood!" With one hand on the child's shoulder and the other resting lightly on the leg below the wound, the mother let the blood trickle over her fingers. Then after a few moments of silence she began to speak, very softly but firmly. "Blood, blood," she said as if continuing the child's cry in another key. "Look how red and strong it is. It is beautiful—it is the most beautiful blood I have ever seen—and it is *your* blood." She was speaking so low the child had to stop screaming to be able to listen —and he wanted to hear more about this most beautiful thing that was *his!* "It is your blood," she continued, "it makes you strong and healthy. Look how it is rushing to your knee to fix it up, so that very soon your wound is all washed and clean. Thank your blood for doing this for you." She paused for a moment. "Now tell your blood you are going to give it good food and good thoughts. . . ."

The loving and intelligent mother realized that washing and bandaging the wound was not sufficient. She made use of an accident, a painful and frightening experience which might easily have been the source of psychological troubles in later life, to teach the child a most important lesson—she made him aware of his own healing power.

A woman came to me worried about her health and her figure. She was selling merchandise by phone, choosing names at random from the telephone book. The irritation of dealing with difficult and elusive clients, plus the unnatural way of communication, plus the fact that her sedentary job prevented her from exercising had reduced the woman to physical and psychological exhaustion. Her breathing was shallow, her circulation poor. "If only I had time to exercise I would be all right," she said.

"How many hours do you spend telephoning?" I asked.

"Six hours a day."

"Splendid," I said. "You have six hours a day to exercise."

And I demonstrated to her how many exercises she could do when telephoning—contraction of muscles of the legs and buttocks, movements of shoulders and arms, exercises for facial and eye muscles, different positions she could take while sitting to stimulate the circulation.

I gave her the recipe, "You Are Not the Target," which relieved a great deal of the exasperation of speaking to disembodied voices, and at times being abused by them.

The first week or two were difficult for her, but after that she went through her work with less and less fatigue, and even rose from her desk refreshed and ready to enjoy her leisure at the end of the day. The exercises and the recipe helped, as they were bound to do, by changing her physical condition and the emotional climate in which she worked. But what probably helped even more was her realization that she was not helpless in her telephonic purgatory! She could do something about the wretched conditions under which she was earning her living: she could *use this!*

It is the very decision to do something about our suffering, the very asking of the question, "HOW CAN I USE THIS?" that begins the conversion of evil into good.

During the last year of the war I was living in Hollywood and playing in the Philharmonic Orchestra in Los Angeles. I had no automobile, and was compelled to travel back and forth on the streetcar a total of two hours a day.

I never had done this before, and I was dismayed. When time is so precious, to pass two hours every day in street-cars! As it turned out, these trolley rides had a vast and beneficial influence in my life because I decided to use that time to study Yoga—at least, as much as could be learned by reading.

It is possible but rare to achieve that state of being in which tragedy—even *our* tragedy—makes sense. But by training our attention, we all can make constructive use of black moods and frustrating circumstances. When we use creative awareness in our daily living we gain these benefits:

We make our mind and our organism more agile and resourceful.

Instead of being the passive victim of a situation we can become its master.

We make the immediate present more endurable.

We fortify ourselves for those possible times when we may confront real misfortune.

Follow these simple directions:

> *Keep yourself constantly reminded, in any way you choose, of the question:*

> ## HOW CAN I USE THIS?

> *Implant the question deep within yourself. Write it on many pieces of paper and keep them in your pocket or*

purse; leave others around, on your dresser, in your car, wherever you are likely to come upon them.

Establish the question in your daily life. Make it one of your habits of mind, so that you will be able, almost automatically, to ask it in those moments when it is necessary.

In time it will become part of your inner world; it will ask itself unconsciously in moments of stress and need.

There is no single answer to the question. The answer depends on the circumstances, and on the intrinsic character of the individual. Very often the recipes in this book will be an answer; at other times the answer will come from other sources.

But this we must remember: *Only if we ask the question will we be given an answer.*

It works—if you work

Let us not talk about the spirit being on one level and the animal on another—let us not separate them, but rather fuse them, use them together, and above all be grateful for both. For were it not for our animal essence we would not be able to perceive the fragrance of a flower—were it not for our spiritual essence we would be incapable of the joy and gratitude that the fragrance of a flower often awakens.

6. DANCE NAKED WITH MUSIC

Go into a room by yourself. Put on your favorite music
Throw off your clothes. And dance.

For one hour, in complete privacy, you are going to be
naked—physically, emotionally, and psychologically.

This may seem to you an extraordinary thing to do. I
agree that most people do not ordinarily shut themselves
into a room and dance naked. Nevertheless, put aside
shyness, reserve, convention—and do this recipe. There
are sound principles behind it, and good values to be
gained from it.

You are going to set your body free of all its limitations
and inhibitions, set it free to feel the music, to move with
it, to be one with it.

This is not an artistic undertaking, so do not judge
yourself. Ignore the mirror, or, if you cannot ignore it,
cover it. Do not correct your movements; do not even allow yourself to make a mental image of your movements.
Do not compare or evaluate—stop judging.

The goal of this dance is not art. The goal is personal
freedom.

Whether you are nineteen or ninety, whether you weigh

one hundred or three hundred pounds, whether you move with ease or difficulty, whether your joints are supple or stiff—no matter. Dance.

This dance is not for anyone's eyes, not even your own.

You are dancing from within, dancing only your feelings, especially your repressed feelings. You are dancing what you cannot tell your mother or father, your husband, lover or friend, what you cannot tell your minister, priest or psychoanalyst, what you cannot tell yourself.

When you are throwing off your clothes, think and feel that you are throwing off all the ideas, feelings, compulsions, embarrassments, fears, and shames that have been *superimposed* upon you. Some of these ideas and restraints are necessary and useful some of the time, but not all of them, and not all of the time. For this dance, throw off everything that has been superimposed upon your real self.

Be whatever you are.

BE—naked and alone.

With the first article of clothing throw off your social status. You may like your status, you may enjoy your social role—no matter. Throw them off.

With the next article of clothing, throw off the blindly accepted conventions of behavior; they may serve you well enough in public. But now, as you get ready to dance, throw them off.

With the third article of clothing, throw off your personal mask, the image of yourself that you present to others. Whatever it is, whether it is an heroic cover for desperation, whether it hides tenderness with a scowl, anxiety with laughter, loneliness with aloofness, resentment with humility—throw it off.

When you come to the last article of clothing, throw off

with it the fear, ignorance, and shame that have been im-
posed upon you by those who lack understanding and respect for sex and love. Throw off that last bit of clothing
and that last restraint before you begin your dance.

If it is loneliness you feel, let all your body feel it. If it
is rage or hostility or fear, feel it with every cell. Through
your naked dance, you expel all the unwanted, painful
feelings.

If these feelings become people and faces and colors,
look at them. If they haunt you, dance them away. Dance
them out, out, out of you.

For one who is an invalid: You can follow the directions
for this recipe, using any part of the body that you can
move. If any part of you is not free to move, follow the
instructions in your imagination. Give a title to your dance
and choose the music. Then close your eyes and dance so
completely in your imagination that you actually feel the
circulation of your blood quickened and stimulated. When,
at the end of your dance, you open your eyes, you will feel
how much more alive, how much more under your control,
and how much more comfortable your body is than before
you did this recipe.

Here is a list of feelings. We experience some of these,
perhaps all of them, at one time or another. Make one of
these the title of your dance or, better, make your own
title.

Dance one of these:

> I am the center of the world, but nobody recognizes it.
> I am afraid, but I don't want anybody to know it.
> I am afraid, but I don't want to let myself know it
> I am afraid in my imagination.

I do to others that which has been done to me.
I must keep up with the Joneses!
I hate the one I love.
I want to give, give, give, but I don't know how.
I am hiding behind myself.
I am hiding behind the devilish part of myself.
I am hiding behind the angelic part of myself.
I am just too tired to dance out my tiredness.
I do not *have* to keep up with the Joneses!

Or of these:

fear—loneliness—injustice—love—anger—
sexual desire—desire to take—desire to give—
apathy—desire to console—desire to hurt—
too afraid to move—hostility—uncertainty—
inability to do what I want—inability to express
myself—or—
I want to love; I want to be loved.
I want to love; I want to be loved.

Listen and be open to the freer part of yourself when you choose or make a title for your dance.

If you are going to dance an unwanted feeling, one that you want to expel and be rid of, continue with your dance until you know that this feeling no longer interferes with you, psychologically or physiologically.

If you choose to dance a feeling that is precious to you, one that makes your life richer, that augments and expands you—then dance it. Let it take hold of you and strengthen your whole organism. Nourish this feeling, and let it bloom like a flower. Let the dance and the music be the sun and the water that nourish this good feeling.

Change the pace of your dance with this VARIATION:

At any point of your dance—suddenly *stop!*

Become a frozen statue.

At any moment, in any position, stop and stiffen. Make your whole body stiff, stiffer, still stiffer. Think of each part of your body and make it stiff.

Keep it stiff as long as you possibly can.

Do not breathe. Your body is so stiff that you cannot even breathe.

You have made your body so stiff that there can be no movement—no movement at all.

When you are at the limit of your endurance, when your body is so absolutely stiff and so absolutely crying for oxygen, when it is humanly impossible to hold it any longer —let go!

You will experience an immense relaxation and with it a flood of gratitude for the enormous privilege of breathing.

Do this several times during your dance. Remember, each time you do it, that your entire body must be stiff, unmoving, like one single piece of ice.

If one could guarantee anything at all in the area of human reactions, I would guarantee that this recipe, properly done, will bring you a period of complete bodily relaxation and pleasurable comfort.

To summarize the directions:

> *Decide the title of your dance.*
>
> *Choose the music.*
>
> *In rhythm with the music, throw off your clothes. With each piece of clothing, throw off a restraint, a convention, a mask imposed upon you by others or yourself.*

Know what each piece of clothing represents. Name it. Know that you are free of it.

Dance. Let the music and your feeling and your body be one. Dance what you feel. BE what you feel. This is your dance. IF you feel like singing—sing. If you feel like shrieking or chanting or wailing, then shriek or chant or wail. This is your dance—your creation—your liberation.

Note: If you do not have a whole hour to dance, then dance for a few minutes, even dressed. Use this recipe whenever you must do something requiring especially controlled behavior; use it before an official function or a difficult interview. If you are going to a party or out with a date, do this recipe. It will freshen and relax you and improve your looks.

It works—if you work

Take this book in small doses. It is better to carry out one
recipe than to read twenty.

7. QUESTIONS AND HOW TO ASK THEM

Scientific research is the art of asking the right question in the right way.

So it is in the exploration of ourselves. It has been said that the right question implicitly contains within itself the right answer, the answer that lies at the center of the problem and will lead to its solution. Each one of us must discover whether this is true.

You may find that you have a question even while you are reading the recipes. You may ask yourself: Where shall I begin? Which recipe is first for me? What is my first, my most urgent need?

It may also happen that a question arises, seemingly from nowhere, while you are carrying out one of the recipes, or perhaps afterwards.

Self-questioning is a first step on the path to self-awareness. And this awareness is a pre-condition for making the most of our lives. It is our protection against unnecessary mental suffering and physical illness, and our aid in coping with these when they cannot be avoided. Being aware is the way toward finding fulfillment in our relationships with others, of bringing all our store of healthy energy to living and working.

A question may be huge and all-embracing: *What do I want out of life?*

Or it may be small, commonplace: What shall I wear today?

No question is trivial. All questions lead to other questions and so, step by step, to the answers. Even the question, Shall I wear the blue dress or the green? may lead to a discovery. The discovery may be that *we cannot even make so small a choice without anxiety.*

And so we have already discovered a deeper question: What is this anxiety that keeps me from deciding what to wear? What or whom do I fear? And why do I rely on so fragile an aid as my dress, to display me, or to hide me?

From this little example alone it is clear that questioning ourselves is not a simple matter, not when we want to receive a real, a living answer, an answer that comes from the whole of our organism. We will call this the *organismic* answer.

In this recipe we shall explore:

> *What questions to ask.*
>
> *How and when to ask them.*
>
> *How the answers may come.*
>
> *How we may recognize an organismic answer.*

At the end of this recipe are a number of possible questions. Each of these questions is both personal and impersonal: personal because it relates to everyone's life; impersonal because, being in a book, it cannot apply to any one person's specific situation. These questions are to help you provide your own question. If the question that comes to you seems superficial or incomplete, pursue it in the ways this recipe suggests, and you will find that it leads you to the fundamental question you are seeking.

Often a question, the first one, is not the real question at all but a substitute which our unconscious self has artfully framed to protect our superficial comfort from being disturbed by a deeper, more troubling doubt.

Why does my wife always want the window closed when she knows I can't sleep unless it is open? I feel I am suffocating. But surely there is enough air in the room! Is it lack of air that keeps me awake? Is it the window? Or is it my attitude toward my wife? The window, open or closed, is a substitute problem. The real problem may be sexual dissatisfaction. Very likely the real question is: How shall I deal with a discontent that is eating its way into my marriage, my happiness, my health?

Sometimes a question reveals not a real but a fancied problem. Why on Sunday night do I lie awake, fearing I will not get up on time for work on Monday morning? I do get up, and I am almost never late for work. What is there about this Sunday night anxiety, so real, so familiar, so old? School! It is a relic of my childhood, an anxiety about school. But I am not a school child any longer. I am grown up, competent, and nothing of real consequence happens if I am late to the office. How to deal with that anxious child that is keeping me awake?

Thus, through questions, we are led to the heart of the matter. We arrive finally at the deep, real question that will take us, like a divining rod, to one or another recipe where we may find an answer.

Each of us must ask his or her own questions. No single

question or set of questions is right for all. Be aware that a question starting with "why" may evoke a conditioned response from the superficial mind. It is from the deeper mind that the new and fresh response applicable to the here and now will come. Phrase your question clearly, and when possible avoid the use of "why."

Choose one question at a time (see page 95). You may wish to write your answer or answers on the blank spaces between the questions. *Date those answers.*

How shall we ask the question, once we have framed it?

It is not enough to ask a question of our conscious self. This is the rational mind, and it is full of rationalizations. It gives us the capacity to deal with our environment, earn our living, study and remember, protect and advance ourselves in the world. Paradoxically, while it endows us with the gifts of deduction and discovery, it often prevents us from discovering ourselves. It is our protective mask, our front, our armor.

Let us remember that we have to pay for the protection that our suit of armor gives us. If a fully armored medieval knight fell from his horse he could hardly get up without assistance. Our armor may make us as stiff and inflexible emotionally. The questions and the recipes are designed to make you able to put your armor off and on at will—to make you able to use your armor *only when necessary* and without becoming paralyzed by its weight and rigidity. Just imagine the prodigious amount of energy spent, generally unconsciously, in carrying around, in holding up, that armor. No wonder we are often inexplicably exhausted!

In the process of protecting us, a suit of armor may, and

generally does, diminish and distort communications with the outer world and the inner world as well. It is true that our armor may protect us from the harshness of some people but it also prevents us from accepting tenderness from some others. It may keep not only our enemies at a distance but our friends and lovers as well. Worst of all, an armor may keep us at a distance from our essential, real self; that essential, real self that now and then—sometimes because of complete love, sometimes suddenly, without obvious reason—we feel in ourselves and perceive in others.

Karen Horney called this "The real self, that central inner force common to all human beings and yet unique to each, which is the deep source of growth." It is from that central force, that part of us that knows, that part of us that has not been touched by pride, prejudice and pain, that we receive inspiration and direction. It is from there that the organismic answer comes.

When we are able to ask questions and receive answers from the real self we need no other techniques. In the meantime we do. Therefore the recipes, the questions, and right now some of the ways in which to ask them.

> *Imagine yourself alone in a mountainous country. Throw your question to the sky and listen to the echo coming back to you from the surrounding crags.*

> *Imagine yourself to be the line of a circumference of an immense circle. Put the question in the center of this circle. Imagine a centrifugal force radiating the question in all directions from the center to its circumference—which is you.*

> *Write your question on several papers and leave them around so that you come across them at various times, when you expect it and when you do not.*

Close your eyes. Visualize a brilliant white wall. Write your question on the white wall. Look at your question. Make it disappear from the wall. Do this five times when you relax during the day or when you go to sleep at night. Look at your question—make it disappear. End this exercise by seeing your question clearly.

Ask your question first thing in the morning when you wake up.

Ask your question rhythmically with a tune when performing some muscular action like walking, exercising, beating eggs, cleaning the house—not when driving.

Dance your question, following the directions given in "Dance Naked with Music."

You surely have seen on the Fourth of July or on other festival occasions wonderful fireworks bursting in all directions and colors in the immense dark sky. To an extent we are like the dark sky, partly mysterious and unperceived..Let the question burst in all directions, exploring and illuminating that part of our inner universe still unrevealed.

Ask your question when resting or daydreaming during the day.

Ask your question when looking in the mirror shaving or making up.

Ask your question to different parts of your body; ask your toes and your spine and your neck. Ask your eyes, your legs, your sexual organs, etc. Every thought and feeling is also a physical happening somewhere in our body. I remember a man, an honest, dedicated minister, who protested over and over that he had forgiven his father for a wrong until I asked him: "Have your guts forgiven him?" He doubled over with an anguishing cramp and shouted: "NO!"

Of these many ways choose one or several which seem most appropriate to you; find other ways.

Continue intense questioning for five or six days. In this period of time you may have several answers; if you have a definite answer, an organismic answer, one that you can act upon, fine. Otherwise drop the question from your conscious mind and let it sink deep in your subconscious. Having asked your question in so many different ways you have implanted it in your many different selves:

In your intellectual self.

In your muscular self, by moving and dancing.

In your physiological self by asking different parts of your body.

In your imaginative self by directing the question to your imagination.

In the twilight region between conscious and unconscious by asking the question as you go to sleep.

And probably in the deeper regions of your unconscious as well.

Ask yourself the question intensely for several days. Then stop asking consciously. Allow the question to go on reverberating through all your being until it evokes a response from your essential self.

When you answer a question do not try to prove anything to yourself or anyone by your answer. You cannot answer freely if you try to prove something. If a question shocks you, amazes you, or arouses any other emotion follow that emotion. Follow that emotion very closely, ride on it as a train rides on its rails: that emotion is part of the answer, your pointer, your guide to it.

Do not expect the answer to come in a neat little pack-

age. Perhaps it will. More often it comes in unexpected
ways. You may suddenly say something that surprises you.
You may awaken one morning with a new feeling, as
though something good had happened to you during sleep.
You may do something completely unexpected. You may
have a strong, significant dream. Or you may have a reaction that illuminates the entire situation for you. For example:

A professional man in his middle thirties was having
difficulty in his relationship with his family. His marriage
was foundering, his wife and children gave him not love
but resentful obedience or open indifference. Yet he loved
his wife and children; all his work, in which he was capable and successful, was dedicated to them. There was a
yawning gap between the love of this man for his family
and his behavior to them, which he described to me with
the deep honesty that springs from necessity. At home he
was dogmatic, domineering, inflexible; it seemed to him
right and proper that to his wife and children he should
behave with unfaltering authority and that he should be
acknowledged as always right.

"Was your father always right?" I interrupted. He
brushed my question aside; he had come not to discuss his
parents, who were very well, but his wife who was always
tired, his children who were growing up without interest
or enthusiasm for anything.

"Whose life are you living?" I asked him suddenly. He
was rather taken aback: his own, of course! What was I
dreaming of? He had good professional standing, a good
home, a wife, children. . . .

We came back at last to the matter of asking oneself

questions. I told him how many interesting ways there are to do it, and for the sake of experiment he agreed to try.

Nothing developed for several days. Then one morning he was shaving. This was a ceremonial; he used an old-fashioned straight razor which his father had long ago given him and taught him how to use. It took him twice as long as most men spend on the task, and he often cut himself. On this morning, however, things were going smoothly; the only difference was that he had been asking himself the preposterous question I had given him: "Whose life am I living?" But just now his mind was wholly absorbed by his shaving. Then, looking in the mirror, his face half white with shaving cream, his hand upraised for the stroke, the revelation came: Father's! It's Father's life I am living!

Father, the man whom, justifiably or not, he had feared and hated throughout his childhood, with whose image he had never come to terms; the harsh justice, the punishments, the decrees promulgated without argument by the man who was axiomatically "always right." Father, who, when his decisions were questioned, would either fly into a rage or withdraw into his study. Father, who complained about the unconscionable amount of work he did for the sake of his ungrateful family.

A sensitive boy, growing up in such an atmosphere, had identified this rigid father as masculine strength and power; he had no other model of manhood. And then, having arrived at manhood with no confidence in his own strength and understanding, he had taken shelter in this hated image, and was wrecking his own and his family's happiness because of it.

For this man, that single question and the revealing "organismic" answer it evoked were enough to break the dam that blocked the free flow of understanding and love.

That was how the answer came to one man. In what way will your answer come to you?

How do we recognize an organismic answer?

My own organismic answer to that question is that I cannot tell you. One can only answer this question for one's self; it is a feeling that must be experienced. Once or perhaps more than once in our lives each one of us has known when something is true, right, complete, when something needed no one's sanction or approval.

The organismic answer may be the first one to emerge, or it may come only after we have shed many answers and questions. Indeed, you may find the first answer destructive and hurtful: never mind. Anger and resentment are human; our inner self is sometimes smothering with the trapped energy of frustrated needs, undisciplined talents, ungratified longings. Choose a recipe that shows you how to make good use of that fundamental energy instead of letting it hurt you or others.

The organismic answer is not easy to describe—scientific or mechanical methods do not apply. At one time what you may consider the organismic answer is easily proved right in the light of facts; at another time it may appear wrong. At one time it may coincide with our obvious present convenience and at another time it points toward upsetting and inconvenient changes. However, the organismic answer has two constant characteristics:

It points to things we—not others—must do or be.

Loudly or softly, it has an uncanny insistence.

If your answer is that change must come from chance or circumstances or from changing someone other than yourself, it is not the organismic answer.

You alone can change yourself, and when you do, then circumstances and people will both seem and *be* changed.

And if some of the questions, mine or your own, are perplexing or disturbing—good, you are ready for action. You will no longer put up with indecision and doubt.

Be impatient.

Begin your questioning NOW.

It works—if you work

When do I do the greatest good to myself?

When do I do the greatest good to others?

When do I do both, giving and receiving at the same time?

What person, real or fictional, impressed me most between the ages of:

five and ten years?

ten and twenty?

twenty and thirty?

Am I today trying to *be* that person?

When do I feel that what I am doing is effortless?

When is it full of effort?

When does the result warrant the effort?

When is it that the performance of my duty gives me a feeling of contentment, serenity, and well-being?

In what ways do my personal education and the culture in which I live restrict me?

In what ways do they enlarge me?

When did I do or say something that was not at all like myself?

Since I was not being myself, who was I being?

Why was I trying to be like that other person?

What do I say I believe—and what do I really believe?

When is it that the physical, mental, and emotional elements of my being are functioning as one whole?

When do I like myself and others best?

Am I able to accept and enjoy an individual completely different from myself—and remain myself completely?

When do I act outwardly as I feel inwardly?

When do I express my real self best?

indequately?

not at all?

When do I feel that I am acting a part written by someone else?

Is my way of looking at the world the only possible way of looking at the world?

Is my reaction to my present situation the only possible reaction I can have to that situation?

When is my reaction to a person or situation spontaneous, complete, *organismic?*

When am I most selfish and most generous at the same time?

Whose life am I living?

What is my ultimate goal in life?

Is what I want now, or what I am doing now, compatible with that goal?

Does the life I am living now make sense?

Tension is largely the result of not knowing how to direct and transform energy. Tension brings illness and suffering. You can absorb the principle of transformation of energy through its many applications in the recipes.

Do the recipes completely; after a while they will become yours!

8. THE ART OF CONVERTING ENERGY

Energy is neither good nor evil. It is a neutral power which can be used well or badly.

The art of living is simply the art of using energy in an intelligent and creative way. The purpose of this recipe is the conversion of energy—its conversion from a neutral power, or from a power that is being used badly, into a beneficent power, directed by intelligence and good will.

This recipe guides you in converting energy by a conscious act of the mind. For this reason it may be more difficult at first than such recipes as "The Tether Ball," "Bubble Freedom," "You Are Not the Target," and others that convert energy directly into physical action. You may want to practice the other recipes first, and then return to this one. When you do, you will find it challenging and rewarding.

The recipe is in five steps, the first of which is basic to the others. In this step, you are asked to make yourself aware of energy as a fundamental, all-pervading force, within you and around you.

You may do this by conscious direction of your imagination, or it may come over you spontaneously in a wave of effortless, intuitive realization. You may have experienced this fundamental energy spontaneously, at some high point in your life.

Wordsworth described it as:

> A sense sublime
> Of something far more deeply interfused,
> Whose dwelling is the light of setting suns,
> And the round ocean and the living air,
> And the blue sky, and in the mind of man . . .

The purpose of the present recipe is to open the door to the experience he expressed in those beautiful lines. Here are the directions:

Choose a comfortable place where you can be alone and undisturbed. Read the directions several times until you feel that you have thoroughly assimilated them. They will be summarized at the end so that you can remember them when you put the book aside.

Become aware of the fundamental energy that is inside your body and all around it.

Think of the pure energy of the sun, of the oceans, of air, water, of the earth itself.

Imagine the enormous amount of pure energy concentrated in one small flower, in one piece of fruit, in a single seed which can become a forest.

What is your favorite form of natural beauty? The mountains? The sea? The graceful movements of a dolphin or of some other animal in its natural state? Think of this form. Let this image fill your mind. Think of the pure impersonal energy contained in it.

Feel the great life-force flowing within and all around you. Feel it in your muscles, in the coursing of your blood, in your entire organism. Let it fill you. Blend with it, until you and energy are one.

In this first step, the aim is not to understand but to feel energy. You may get this feeling immediately, or it may take a little practice. This one step alone is a wonderful energizer.

Now turn this experience of energy into a specific personal form.

Relive a moment when you were filled with an awareness of energy, vitality, life force, in a good and happy personal experience.

Recall a moment of great joy and harmony, of strength, or powerful creative energy. It may have been when you were walking freely in a forest or on a beach or when you were winning a contest; when you accomplished a difficult task acknowledged by many, or performed an humble but arduous chore unrecognized by any. It could be the moment when you first bite into a succulent piece of fresh fruit—or that moment when you are ready for, and know you are going to have, a fulfilling experience in love. It may be when you are doing absolutely nothing, and nothing extraordinary is happening, nothing except that you are aware of the ongoing miracle of energy flowing within you.

Relive your own experience, that moment when your whole being was swept and your vitality intensified by a wave of fluid, creative energy.

Relive it completely.

Now turn quickly to a moment when energy was destructive to you.

This may have been a moment when you experienced physical injury, when you saw someone else experience physical injury, a time when something precious to you was destroyed, a time when destructive energy was flung at you or others in words or actions, a time when destructive energy was silently communicated through ugly thoughts and emotions.

Choose one such incident out of your life.

Relive it.

Feel it. Do not just remember it.

Feel the impact of this destructive energy as you felt the inspiring flow of creative energy.

Let the feeling rise slowly in you. Or, if this comes more natural to you, let yourself be engulfed by it, in an instant. Relive the incident from its very beginning to the final climactic moment of its destructive fulfillment.

When you have felt, completely and separately, these three forms of energy: impersonal energy, creative personal energy and destructive personal energy—you are ready for the fourth step.

Now you are going to alternate step two and step three.

Once more, let yourself feel that moment of personal creative energy.

Then, immediately, replace that feeling with the experience of destructive energy.

Let yourself go into the happy emotion; then switch into the bad one. Feel each of these experiences completely. Do not merely recall the events, but feel them totally, all the emotions, all the physical sensations.

For practice, it may help to visualize sharply contrasting colors: black and white, or red and green. Visualize white totally. Then quickly replace it in your mind's eye with black. Do the same exercise with sound, filling your ears with an imagined high, thin note, then replacing it with a deep, full bass note.

Now alternate your two opposite experiences of energy: the happy, creative moment—feel it completely; then the unhappy, destructive moment—feel that also, totally, in mind and body.

Practice until you can swing back and forth between these two extremes in the experience of personal energy. The important thing is to learn to alternate quickly these opposite sensations, the total feeling of good with the total feeling of the bad, not the mere recollection of the events.

Repeat the preceding step. Swing back and forth once more between the two opposites of energy: creative and destructive, good and bad.

Now, quickly, by a conscious direction of your whole being, extract the good feelings from the creative experience and the bad feelings from the destructive experience—and float into the experience of pure impersonal energy as you did in the first step.

With full awareness, know that you are drawing out the good and the bad, the personal elements of each experience, and that you are letting yourself be engulfed by the impersonal flow of fundamental energy.

When you are able to do this well, you will find that you have gained remarkable power to direct your internal and external life.

Here is a summary of the directions to help you to remember them.

Experience pure energy.

Experience personal creative energy.

Experience personal destructive energy.

Experience in rapid alternation:
   Personal creative energy, then
   Personal destructive energy.

Repeat the last step, then rapidly return to the first.

Be sure always to end this recipe with the first step: fundamental energy.

By daily practice, you can become a CONSCIOUS AND INTELLIGENT DIRECTOR OF ENERGY.

In your daily life, in the midst of business, chores, activities—stop: and for just a few moments, experience pure impersonal energy.

Feel it.

And discover that *"Energy Is Eternal Delight."*

It works—if you work

In daily living often you have to control your emotions: it may be dangerous, impractical, or cruel to express all you feel in your social or family situation. But when you are alone and doing the recipes—feel. Feel to the limit.

9. LOVE YOURSELF AS YOU LOVE YOUR NEIGHBOR

It is almost as destructive *not* to respect and love oneself as it is to respect and love *only* oneself.

This is destructive because it generates energy directed against the life that is constantly present and flowing within us. It is doubly damaging; for we are both the hangman and his victim.

It is harmful to reject a human being; it is harmful to be rejected. When we do not respect or love ourselves we commit both offenses.

Erich Fromm summed up the matter in this way: "If it is a virtue to love my neighbor as a human being, it must be a virtue—and not a vice—to love myself, since I am a human being too. There is no concept of man in which I myself am not included."

What brings about self-rejection?

There are many causes; one of the most significant is that many people reject themselves for the illogical but emotionally compelling reason that they were once rejected by someone else.

These especially momentous rejections take place very early in life, usually even before the child can put his

thoughts and feelings into words. Words come later, and
they come only to those who have looked deeply enough
into themselves to discover why it is that they dislike themselves. The words may come in some such form as this:

> As a child I was rejected, or felt I was, by someone
> from whom I expected and needed love. The most
> powerful person in my small universe, the supremely
> important person who was taking care of me and on
> whom I depended absolutely, was angry with me, per-
> haps even punished me.
>
> That person, whether mother, father, aunt, nurse, or
> any adult who had charge of me, was a giant in my
> world, the all-knowing, all-powerful controller of my
> destiny. The giant could give or withhold food, comfort,
> warmth, love. When the giant was angry, my whole
> world trembled. When the giant said that I was bad,
> I WAS BAD.
>
> How can I not be bad if the giant says I am? The
> giant punishes me—the punishment is real—usually my
> buttocks bear witness to its reality. Therefore (such is
> the logic of feeling) everything the giant does is real,
> everything the giant says is true. He says that I am bad,
> so I am bad.
>
> I could not know that sometimes the giant was tired,
> or anxious, or ill, and therefore less gentle and loving
> with me. I could not know that the giant was also trying
> to teach me what I must know to live in the world.
> Sometimes when my tummy rumbled and something of
> my own creation came out of it, the giant was happy and
> praised me. But another time, when the same thing
> happened, the giant was angry, and scolded and pun-
> ished me. Yet inside I felt just the same.
>
> It seemed to me that if I could be powerful like the
> giant, I would be safe. And so, in childish fantasy, I took
> on the most impressive of the giant's characteristics: his
> power, and his disapproval of the bad child—myself.

Rejection of oneself most often begins in infancy, in those early years when the need for nourishment and physical love is at its highest, when the behavior of adults is utterly mysterious, when everything that happens seems to be aimed directly at oneself, the egocentric little being whose own pleasure and pain constitute the whole of his universe. The logic, to the primitive infant mind, is faultless:

I depend upon the giant.

The giant disapproves of me.

I try to be like—indeed, to *be*—the giant.

Like the giant, I must disapprove of myself.

Or, to put it another way: if this powerful, all-knowing being finds me unworthy of love, then I must be unworthy of love, my own or any other's.

You may feel that this recipe is not for you, and perhaps it is not. Nevertheless, give it a trial. It may enable you to discover interesting and important facts about yourself.

Regardless of the special content of this recipe, the psychophysical exercise that forms the second part of the recipe is of value to everyone. It is one of the most powerful energizers for mind and body. Here are the directions:

The first part of this recipe is the following question.*
Who do I feel does not love me?

You may have a sudden clarifying answer, or you may have to remain with the question for days or even weeks. The question may bring to the surface considerable emotion: experience it; do not try to manipulate it, judge it, repress it, or rationalize it away. An incident of the past, recent or remote, may emerge. Do not push it aside. It may

* Refer to the recipe "Questions and How to Ask Them" and follow those directions.

be your open door to understanding and liberation. Sometimes it is painful to go through that door, but go through it none the less. The reward will greatly compensate you for the effort. It is not by keeping pain locked up in us that we become free and well; it is by getting the pain out of our system. Thus we liberate the energy encapsulated in it, and can use that energy for our own and others' benefit.

Whatever your reaction to the question, however long it takes you to find the answer, do not fail each time to follow a period of asking with this psychophysical exercise:

Choose a quiet place where you can concentrate undisturbed.

Find a comfortable position, sitting or lying down.

Now, in any order you prefer, be fully conscious of

neck	shoulders	arterial system
ear	saliva	pelvic muscles
eyes	left lung	upper legs
blood	toes	intestinal tract
hair	gums	right lung (Etc.)

For reasons both mental and physical, it is most helpful, in fact generally necessary, to place your hand or hands on that part of your body with which you are communicating.

Say, do, think whatever is most effective in making you completely aware of that part of your body.

Send an energy wave or a love thought to that part of your body. Talk to it, imagine that it has become filled with luminous radiant energy, feel it growing warm, feel it tingling and pulsing with life.

Experiment, find out for yourself the best way for you to become most aware of that part of your body. Discover how, for a few seconds or minutes, you can actu-

ally be that part of your body. Be your neck. Be your eyes. Be the big toe of your right foot.

This is a most valuable discipline. Whether you like yourself too little, too much, or just enough, practice it as often as you can, if possible for a half hour at a stretch. At the end of each period you will feel more alive and very likely more respectful of the marvel of your body, more impressed by what the friendly collaboration between your body and you can do.

After you have asked the leading question and perhaps found a piece, or all, of the answer, after you have performed the psychophysical exercise that follows it, end this recipe in this way:

> Make a mental inventory of your assets, particularly of those that you are in the habit of overlooking.
>
> Are you making the most of them?

It works—if you work

Sometimes we know why a recipe makes us feel better. At other times the reason for our improvement remains mysterious. Our body-mind is so much vaster than our "presumptuous brain" * can measure, so much more resourceful. It knew how to steer us to survival, eons before the computing part of our brain, the cortex, began its fabulous development.

When we are better—let us be better.

When we do not know why—let us delight and trust in the mystery.

* See Albert T. W. Simeons' excellent book, *Man's Presumptuous Brain*, Dutton, 1961.

10. GO WITH IT

In most situations in our lives we feel we must do something, take control, manage. Or at the least, we must make our wishes known. We must be clear in our own minds about what we want, and make this clear to others. If we do not, and things turn out badly, then we feel, and quite rightly, that we have only ourselves to blame.

The purpose of many of these recipes is to redirect energy. The aim of this one is to *go with it*.

Some situations are beyond our control. We see this most clearly in the relationship between parents and children. For years a parent takes responsibility for the child, makes the decisions, guides him, and tries with more or less success to direct the thinking and emotional development of the child. This is what we understand as the parent's role. But there comes a time when it is important, indeed essential, to set the child free. There comes a time when the child is an adult, and must take over responsibility for his or her own fate. This does not come all at once, but gradually through the years. Yet to parents it often appears as a sudden cruel stroke of the sword severing a long-standing and cherished relationship. We cannot change the fact that time passes and, as it passes, children cease to be children.

When circumstances are changeable we have many choices. When they are unchangeable our only choice is to accept them with good grace or accept them with poor grace. In this recipe we are dealing with the situation in which we have chosen not to resist but to gracefully *go with it.*

There are many situations in which it is not important to resist, not important to have one's own way; situations in which it is good to yield to the other's wish, good to *go with it.*

The ability to be passive, then, is also one that we need to cultivate.

The art of being passive by choice, the ability to *go with it,* is the purpose of this recipe.

Can you remember an occasion when you did what someone else wanted, simply because it was asked of you? An occasion when you had a feeling of going with the wish of another? We are not speaking here of:

Grim determination: *I'll give him his way, and show him how wrong he is.*

Duty: I have no choice; *this is my duty as a daughter (son, wife, husband,* etc.).

Martyrdom: *I must sacrifice myself for his (her) sake.*

Reward: *If I do this, he (she) will recognize and value my devotion.*

Appeasement: *If I do this, I will not be punished.*

"Go with it" involves none of the above. It means only an easy, comfortable acceptance of going along with another person's wish.

Can you remember one such occasion?

If you have never had the experience of graceful, comfortable passivity, then it is time you began. There is a place for passivity in all our lives.

It should not become a habit. There are times to take a stand, make an issue, resist with all our strength. Going with it is not a way of life!

Even for the outwardly passive person, this recipe may be illuminating, for his passivity may be only skin deep. Beneath the surface there may lurk elements of those feelings that we have listed above: grimness, a sense of duty, martyrdom, a wish for reward, a wish to appease. At other times there is a mistrust in one's own capacity, a deep seated indecision, a sense of inferiority. Accompanying these feelings often there is also resentment and depression. Do not mistake these for the simple decision to be passive and unresisting, to go with another's wish on occasion.

Examine yourself. Consider whether, in going with it, you have felt easy and comfortable. Or did you feel angry, resentful, or depressed?

Either way, you can benefit by this recipe. Here are the directions:

Imagine a quiet, peaceful, gentle river. It flows evenly and smoothly over a pleasant sandy bed without boulders, without impediments—an even, gentle flow over the countryside, cool but not cold.

Step into the river.

Let yourself go.

Float with it.

Float.

No responsibility, no action.

Simply go with the flow of the river.

Smoothly float.

Now re-live a past contrasting situation where you had to do something against your wishes. Feel the situation, the other person's attitude.

Feel your resistance to that person or situation. Feel it in your body-mind, wherever it is located.

Now feel yourself effortlessly floating on the peaceful river. Go with it.

Now re-live the same past contrasting situation in this way: do not fight your resistance to the person or situation, do not try to change your opinion, your conviction, but simply put them aside for a little while, firmly and gently.

Realize, in every way that you can, the difference between fighting, overcoming a resistance, changing an opinion, and just putting them aside for a while. When you give resistance and opinion your attention, you give them life. Deprive them of that life.

Also realize that this has nothing in common with the feeling of "giving up." One usually gives up because one is too tired or discouraged to do anything else. "Going with it" is different. You decide to do it, with the full capacity of your intelligence and will.

Do this several times:

Feel the pleasant, smoothly floating river.

Feel your resistance to a past uncomfortable situation, person, atmosphere.

> Then, the situation unchanged, you change, by floating
> with it, by reliving it with the river feeling.

Do this in the privacy of your room when you take a rest,
or when you go to sleep.

When you have learned to do it well, apply it to life.
Naturally you are the only one who knows which are the
situations and personal relationships in which it is advisable to "go with it." However I suggest doing it at first
with little, annoying, apparently unimportant circumstances. On these occasions you can alternate this recipe
with "You are Not the Target."

Little chores, little irritations, sometimes little people
—simply float with them. You will be surprised how often
they start floating with you.

In more important situations, first decide whether this
is a time for resistance or for acceptance, for going against
it or going with it. As with little things, you may be surprised to find how often big things also begin floating with
you, floating smoothly with the deep flowing life of the
river.

It works—if you work

Let us direct the floodlight of our awareness to our blind spots. The necessity is to become aware of what escapes our awareness. And again to become aware of what eludes us. And again. And again.

11. TO HELL WITH CAUTION

(specially dedicated to those over forty)

"Be careful, be careful, be careful!" we were told hundreds of times during our childhood. "Be careful, be careful, be careful!" we repeat hundreds of times to our children, to our grandchildren. And the suggestion, "Be careful!" becomes more and more deeply grooved in our unconscious minds. It acts with the force of a post-hypnotic suggestion, making us automatically, often blindly and unnecessarily cautious.

Some degree of caution is of course necessary for survival; it would be utter folly to suggest that we abandon entirely all common sense and good judgment. These are realistic and rational; they deal with the situation as it exists in reality. The caution we would throw to the winds is a generalized, diffuse atmosphere of caution, a fog of carefulness that obscures reality and beclouds reason. Very often it leads us in the opposite direction from common sense and real security.

There is physical caution and psychological caution. They are not neatly divided. Suppose I am cautiously speaking on the phone to someone who I am afraid will fly into a rage. I have nothing to fear physically, yet my body is tense and uneasy because it reflects my psychological cautiousness. Likewise when I am physically cautious my mind participates in that feeling.

We pay a psychological and physical price for habitual overcaution. Being too careful, being constantly afraid, suspicious, secretive—these feeling-patterns produce a continuous inner tension. And this tension in turn constricts the circulation of ideas, of feelings, even of life-giving blood. Habitual caution ties and binds us; it is as if we were dressed always in clothes and shoes that were several sizes too small.

Let us examine the anatomy of caution. Its two main motivations are survival and fear. If I am careful when I cross the street in traffic I perform an action necessary to my survival. If I am equally hesitant and watchful, even after I have assured myself that *the street is empty,* then I am not careful but fearful. Although my survival is not threatened, still something within me makes me behave as though it were. Automatically I am protecting myself against an imagined danger.

There is a difference between voluntary, clear-minded caution and caution that is involuntary, automatic, and obsessive. Watch the cautious movements of a young cat in a new situation. What you see is controlled grace, intelligence, quickness; the animal is alert; it is alive. Watch the neurotically cautious person: he is stiff, awkward, slow; he is tense, and therefore he is clumsy, and his caution is actually self-defeating, because the clumsiness that results from it is as likely to produce an accident as to avoid one. The young animal's caution is a realistic response to an immediate survival situation here and now. The neurotic's caution is a response to a danger that may have been real in the past, or a reaction to a verbal command given years ago, yet he still behaves as though they were threatening and commanding him *now*.

Secrecy is another form of caution—At times it is essential. But often people are crippled by the feeling or belief that something must be kept hidden or the consequences would be disastrous! How often is this true?

A woman came to speak to me. She said it was about something very important and strictly private. There was something furtive about her way of moving and talking. Her posture, her whole being, seemed bent to cover a secret. She had come to tell me—but she could hardly do so.

She began to speak, in a low voice, carefully observing my every reaction; then, as though a dam had been broken, her words came more and more rapidly as she recounted an unfortunate incident that had happened twenty years ago three thousand miles away. A close relative had been involved in a scandal which, for a couple of days, had made news in the local paper of her little town. She had left town long since but whenever anything adverse happened to her this hunted woman was persuaded that her dark secret had come to light again. When she lost a job she changed location because "everybody there knew about it." Every relationship was clouded with continuous apprehension. She felt better for telling me. But she made a remarkable change only when she realized that it was now of no interest or consequence what had happened to her relative twenty years ago. Everyone noticed how the posture, the voice, the figure of this woman had changed. It was as though she had thrown away a dead weight. She did in fact lose a considerable amount of excess weight.

It often happens that when the parents are overcautious

their children will find themselves in exactly the kind of difficulty they have been warned against: "Be careful, you are going to fall!" "Be careful, you are going to catch cold!" and the child duly falls; the child catches the predicted cold. There are two main causes for this. One is the parents' overcautiousness which infects the child with their own fear; the other is the disturbed response of the child to this fear coming from the very persons from whom he expects courage and strength.

Imagine a five-year-old child running happily and lightly, and a father exclaiming over and over, "Look out! Watch yourself now! Be careful—you're going to fall!" The father, in his forties, possibly overweight, with muscles flabby and joints stiff from sedentary living, imagines himself running like his child across the gravel, running and falling—ouch! But the child has the natural coordination of youth and health, and in addition he is not fearful. If he does fall he will not fall far, and probably he will not suffer more than a skinned knee. But with his father's warning in his ear he stiffens, loses his easy coordination; his father's prediction proves correct. He does fall, and the pattern of "Be careful, you'll fall!" begins to wear its pathway in his unconscious mind. Gone is the natural grace, the coordinated movement, the effortless alertness to impediments that may trip him. He is doomed to fall, and to be everlastingly afraid of falling. How much better if the watchful parent kept his fears to himself, used good sense in choosing where and when his child could run freely, and then let him run, even let him fall! The minor bumps and bruises are a learning experience; a child who has fallen a little is learning to move with the skill that saves him from falling.

We cannot make rules as to when caution is good sense and when it is neurotic fearfulness. Each situation has its own rules for each individual.

Consider a hostess, a new bride, giving her first party. She looks over her table setting a dozen times, rehearses her plans for serving and clearing, tastes the casserole again and again. Will there be enough? Should she have ordered more ice? Will her mother-in-law or her husband's boss be sufficiently impressed? What if she should spill something, break something! Like the young animal in an unfamiliar situation, she is understandably tense and nervous. She will not enjoy her party; its end will come only as a relief.

Now imagine the same hostess twenty years later. Imagine her going through the same tense, nervous ritual, the same fearful premonitions of disaster. Imagine her enjoying her guests just as little, welcoming the end of her party with the same deep sigh of relief. After twenty years and probably hundreds of parties, after many experiences as hostess and as guest observing other hostesses, she still goes through this now meaningless series of painfully cautious, needlessly self-protective acts.

A brilliant motion picture director was telling me the exasperating consequences that overcautiousness occasionally has on the complicated work of filming a picture. Besides the actors, this work requires the coordination of many highly paid, specialized technicians. Many things can go wrong and it is all too easy to make costly mistakes. Jobs are few and much sought after. It is not surprising therefore that the atmosphere on a Hollywood set is often agonizingly tense. "Today everybody was so nervous," my friend told me, "that I announced I would give a prize to anyone who made a mistake and said so at once. Instantly the atmosphere changed—everybody did his work better and quicker; and there was a good feeling all around. A few mistakes occurred, but because they were immediately admitted they could be corrected on the spot. Often we see mistakes days later when the film comes back from the laboratory and it is too late or too expensive to correct them."

This very intuitive director knew that by making people free of overcautiousness he was actually improving the quality of work.

It is to those over forty that this recipe is especially dedicated. The power of habit increases with time, the power of suggestion in proportion to the number of repetitions. If we have been careful since childhood, by the age of thirty we will probably be very careful, and by forty we are extremely careful. Unless we do something about it, each year the habit and the suggestion become more firmly implanted and we become more restricted in body and mind.

Few experiences are as renewing and rejuvenating as throwing the dead weight of caution to the wind at the right time. The way in which each of us chooses to do this is highly personal, but the opportunities are everywhere. Some do it by seeking new experiences and adventures. A woman I know in her sixties took a trip to Alaska; this in itself was no act of daring because she went on a conducted tour. But at its northernmost point she left the tour. Since she was so far north, she decided that she would once in her life step within the Arctic Circle, to see, smell, feel the impact of that frozen top of the world. There were no accommodations; she had to sleep on an improvised cot in the radio shack. But she saw the Arctic, its brilliant sky and its glistening icy sea, and she came back renewed and refreshed, not only with the experience itself but with the sense of freedom her own act of daring had given her.

Many men and women in their senior years are embarking on even more daring adventures. Not all of us over forty are in the privileged position of being able to abandon our present way of life and go on to something totally new, like the service members of the peace corps. Not all of us can learn new skills such as skiing or parachute jumping, or fire walking—but we can all find in our everyday lives many opportunities to throw caution to the winds. This does not mean becoming reckless and causing accidents to ourselves and others.

It does mean becoming aware of and getting rid of automatic, restricting, useless overcautions that have been with us too long. It does mean that we can start developing some of those latent potentialities which, when we were beginning a career or rearing a family, we had to neglect. Think of all the things you wanted to do and have never done. Some of them are possible today.

If you object, "But I have never done that before!" then, may I say, so much more reason for starting now! It is very interesting and sometimes revealing to observe what goes on inside of us when we repeat that over-used phrase, "I have never done that before!"

To free you from the chains of useless overcaution, here are the directions:

> Consider a situation in which you are especially careful. Are you always cautious in the same situation? Were your parents cautious in a similar situation? Consider

how you yourself ordinarily move, and then imagine yourself moving, talking, being, in that particular situation. Is there any difference? Do you feel restraint, constriction in your muscles, in your movements?

Consider the things you so carefully hide: is it necessary to keep them secrets? It may have been necessary at some time in your life, but is it necessary now? Consider the energy you use and the tension produced in yourself for the purpose of secrecy. Ask yourself:

Would knowing your secret change someone's attitude toward you?

Would letting go of some secret relieve some of your tension?

On the next page is a list of words which arouse cautious feelings in many of us.

Read the list slowly to yourself.

Read it aloud.

Add your own caution signals if they are not on the list.

When one of these words brings a reaction, however vague, even if it is only a feeling of discomfort and constriction, stop, and locate the feeling immediately in your body.

Now please turn the page.

Health	Husband	Old age
Security	Children	Marriage
Food	New acquaintances	Atom bomb
It is a secret	Business decisions	Ability
Men	Going on a journey	Driving
Women	Coming home	Draft
Sex	Employee	Eating
Money	Automobiles	Drinking
Employer	Airplanes	Boss
Mother	Electricity	God
Religion	Relatives	Freedom
Father	Work	Change
New places	Groups	Elevators
Wife	Weight	Run
New skills	Loneliness	Go back

For every emotion there is a physical response, but sometimes it is not easy to locate. The bodily changes in response to emotions are different for each individual. Your response to overcautiousness may be in one of these areas:

Solar plexus	All over the body	Legs
Neck	Intestinal tract	Throat
Forehead	Shoulders	Eyes
Jaw	Tongue	Head
Feet		

It is likely that more than one area is involved, and perhaps other areas not listed here.

> Choose one part of your body, the one of which you are most aware, and work on that part.

> If you cannot find a place in your body that responds to one of the words or ideas on the list, imagine it. What muscle or organ or system in your body may be affected

by these feelings? Follow the directions with that part. The recipe is just as effective when you work with your imagination.

If it is a part of your body which cannot be exercised or of which you know you should be careful (should you?) concentrate intensely on that area of your body, send a thought of energy to it, until you feel it tingling and warm.

If it is a part of the body that can be exercised, alternate these two exercises:

Make that part of your body very stiff, and hold the stiffness as long as you can.

Let go.

Move that part of your body; move it as fast as you can.

While you do these physical exercises, visualize the caution, the tension, the secrecy, the fears.

See them dropping out, dripping out, shaken out of that part of your body, like unclean water being squeezed, wrung, shaken out. See this clearly in your mind's eye; the clearer the image, the better the result.

Synchronize meaningful physical activity with sharp visualization. Out, out, shake out the cloudy, muddy water, squeeze it out as you stiffen and let go, shake it out as you move and shake those muscles, squeeze and shake and drive out the opaque water.

Do this for several minutes or as long as you can.

Now place yourself in a comfortable position, close your eyes, and think intensively of that part of your body. Visualize it clearly.

Imagine a mountain stream of cool, fresh, limpid water flowing through that part. Feel the water give it freshness, freedom, vitality. Feel this as deeply as you can; the deeper the feeling, the better the results.

There are two ways of ending this recipe.
Either:

Continue to see and feel the clear vitalizing water flowing through that part of your body, and fall asleep with the image.

Or:

Get up and dance. Give your dance the title: "To Hell with Caution." Follow the directions for the recipe, Dance Naked with Music.

It works—if you work

Those who are rich in feeling are often also vulnerable: a word, an inflection, a silence, a gesture, even a color or sound is felt as hurt, pain, offense. These richly endowed but vulnerable people are on the horns of a dilemma. If they fail to protect themselves they suffer acutely. But if they protect themselves in the ordinary way—by suppressing all feelings, by encasing themselves in the armor of indifference or cynicism—they separate themselves from the very source of life. The recipes offer a way between the horns of the dilemma.

12. ATTEND YOUR FUNERAL

Read this recipe a few times until you are well acquainted with its sequence. Then lay aside the recipe and experience it.

It may seem to you a very strange recipe. Yet it is not so strange. Most of us have said to ourselves at some time, usually in childhood, *If I were dead they would be sorry!* Some of us played out the fantasy as a game, imagining ourselves dead, imagining our parents weeping. It served us then; a wholesome device for the release of childhood frustrations. It can serve us now as adults.

Be sure that you will be alone for about two hours. Make certain there will be no telephone calls, bells, or other interruptions.

Have the room comfortably dark or dimly lighted.

Lie down on your bed or sofa or on the floor.

Let your body go. Imagine that the life is out of it. Do not speak or move.

Imagine that you have died. Your body is passive, lifeless, useless. Your body is discarded. Your funeral is about to take place.

You are now going to your own funeral.

Look at the people who have come to your funeral. What do they feel? How do they look at your body? Do they need consolation? Are they happy to be alive? Would *they* like to be dead? What are their emotions?

Look at the people coming to say a last goodby to this discarded body. Look at each of them. Is there one among them to whom you would like to say something, to explain something, to express a certain feeling? You cannot do it. Without your power of speech, of writing, of moving —without your body you can do nothing.

Look again at the people who attend your funeral. What would you like to say to each of them, if you could speak? How would you express yourself to this or that person, if you had a body?

If looking at someone at your funeral makes you want to cry—then do cry, deeply and freely. You have every right to your tears.

Do you have a problem which has been difficult to solve? Do you have a decision which has been difficult to make? Your problem, your decision will most probably be clarified at this moment.

Did you look at the flowers people sent you? What kind are they? How many are there? Did the people try to suit the preferences of the person you were? Or did they only do what they thought they ought to do?

Is anyone giving the eulogy? What is he saying? Does it seem to you sensible, reasonably true to you and your life?

Is there music? Has someone chosen it who knew what you liked, what you would prefer?

Now turn your attention to the person whom you disliked or hated or who irritated or repelled you more than any other in your life. Is there anything you want to say to that person?

Say it.

And now look at the one or ones you love most, at the one or ones to whom you are most grateful. Say whatever you wish or feel like saying. If tears do not let you speak, continue to cry and try to say what you feel.

This is your last party. Speak to everyone there, tell them all about yourself, about your mistakes and your suffering, about your love and your longings. No longer do you need to protect yourself, no longer do you need to hide behind a wall or a suit of armor. It is your last party: you can explode, you can be miserable or pitiful, insignificant or despicable. At your funeral you can be yourself.

> And now it is over. Come back to your living body.
> Acknowledge it and respect it. Feel the life flowing in it.
> Wriggle your toes.
> Stretch your arms.
> Blink your eyes.
> Rotate your head.
> Direct your attention to the circulation of your blood.
> Feel your heart beat.
> Say your name aloud.
> Now sit up.
> With your hands, gently touch different parts of your body.
> Look at the room about you. Notice ten objects in the room.
> Verify what day it is, and what time of day.
> Swallow three times.
> Stretch and feel your live body. Get up and move about.
> Feel how your body moves.

Look at something beautiful.
Smell something you like.
Touch something you like.
Clap your hands five times.
Bite into a fresh fruit. Chew a long, long time.
Do once quickly the recipe "Lay the Ghost."

Now:

Take a paper and pencil and make a list of the things you wanted to say or do when you had no body with which to speak or act.

Read the list.
Choose two items which appear most constructive to
  you.
Begin to do them.
Begin now.

It works—if you work

"What is the point of all this?" *we ask when life seems cruel, illogical, incomprehensible. Life often gives a clarifying answer.*

"What is the point of all this?" *you may ask when a recipe seems cruel, illogical, incomprehensible. One could offer a whole series of answers: psychological, physiological, philosophical, what you will—but such answers would be beside the point. These recipes are for you, for* your better living and loving. *So what is the point of all this? The point is to find* your *answer.*

13. ATTEND YOUR FUNERAL ALONE

Some of us believe we are—or imagine we are—completely unloved. It is possible. If sometimes you feel this way, imagine that at your funeral there is no one.

Before going to your lonely funeral, make yourself very comfortable and make certain you are not going to be interrupted by people or the telephone or other distractions for about two hours.

Let go of your body. Let it be there as something which is no longer yours. Abandon it for a while. Take your attention completely away from your living body. Attend your funeral. Look at the room or the place where your lifeless body is; you are there alone, at your lonely funeral. Perhaps there was no one in your life; there is no one in your death.

If this is so, if it really is so, then follow whatever feeling such a situation produces in you. There it is, your dead body, and no one cares. Follow to the limit this feeling of being completely alone, abandoned, not loved—not in life, not in death. Follow this feeling; cry, scream, curse, if you feel like it.

Cry, scream, curse, if this is what you feel. Go to the limit of your feeling. And after you have cried and screamed and cursed, when you are empty and exhausted, stop and listen.

This is your chance: do what others have failed to do. Look at the unloved one, the miserable one. This is your chance to do an act of love toward one who has had no love. This is your chance to do justice where intentional or un-intentional injustice has been committed.

This is your chance to give warmth and courage to one who feels only coldness, loneliness and death. This is your chance to change those bitter downward lines in that life-less face, your chance to smooth them out. This is your chance, your first step toward love; give it to this unloved one. Give love to one who has forgotten what love is, to one who feels he has never known it.

Let your tears flow from the very depth of you. Let your bitterness flow out with them. And when the bitterness is out, your tears will be gentle and sweet. Then take the hand of this lifeless body of yours, take it in your hands and with respect and love bring it to your lips and kiss it.

Now gently come back to your living body.

With this feeling of respect and love, come back to your living body, and let this feeling remain with you, inside of you. Let it spread to each nerve, to each muscle, along every vein and artery. Let this feeling of respect and love spread inside you, throughout your entire organism, and then let it spread out around you in everything, object or animal or human, that is part of your life. Feel this feeling of love and respect circulating inside you with the force of life itself; let it be in your blood, in the air you breathe. Feel it—accept it—give it.

Do the recipe "Lay the Ghost, or Here and Now."

It works—if you work

Problems and suffering, restlessness, loss of interest, bore-dom—at times all of these are protests of your deeper self. These protests, loud and clamorous or soft, obscure, and elusive, can be the very stimulus for the development of your unrealized creative potentials. Listen to those protests and use them as incentives.

14. BUBBLE FREEDOM

Here we are dealing not with major events but with large and small annoyances that arise so often between employer and employee, salesman and client, driver and policeman —and between those who love each other and yet constantly manage to get on each other's nerves.

This recipe is not only an excellent method for dealing with such irritating episodes; it is also remarkably effective in refreshing and beautifying. Try it when you are about to go out for a date. It often works wonders.

> Take a bowl of cold water large enough for your face; put in a few cubes of ice.
>
> Take a pail or bucket that will hold water knee-deep (a plastic wastepaper basket will do) and fill it with hot water. This is for your feet.
>
> As you make these preparations, think of whatever may be troubling you. It may be a small thing for someone else but not for you. It annoys you; you would feel freer if it were not there. Do not try to reason yourself out of it. Simply remember it. Feel it. Keep it present while you prepare for this recipe. Get out the pail, the bowl. Fill one with hot, one with cold water.

Put the ice cubes in the cold water. As you do these things, feel your troubling incident. Feel its unpleasantness.

Feel it all the while you make your arrangements and choose where you will do this recipe. Your bathroom is good; your kitchen is also good; any place that has privacy and comfort is good.

Keep the incident in your mind while you take off your shoes and stockings.

Think of it, feel its unpleasantness, while you place the bowl with the cold water and ice cubes on a table or counter and the bucket of hot water on the floor.

Step into the hot water, up to your calves or knees.

Take a deep breath and plunge your whole face into the bowl of cold water.

Hold your breath as long as it is comfortable.

Let your lips loosen and relax. Through your relaxed lips bubble your breath into the water.

Raise your face and take a deeper breath. Again, immerse your face in the water, holding your breath just a little longer than is comfortable.

As you hold your breath in the cold water, think and feel that unpleasantness. Perhaps it was an occasion when you would have liked to say something short and sharp and biting. But you did not, because words failed you, because you were not given a chance to speak, or because you would have hurt someone or would have been hurt by speaking. Think, now, of that unspoken phrase.

After holding your breath—and the words—let them out, with lips loose and relaxed under the water.

Let the bubbles be your unspoken irritation, your righteous protest, your frustrated silence, your final word.

Now raise your head and take another breath through your nose.

This time, hold it even longer than the preceding one. Hold it until it is uncomfortable.

Plunge your face into the water.

Let out the breath. Bubbling with your lips loose and relaxed, make as much noise as possible.

Those bubbles are talking for you.

With your face immersed in the water, bubble out any noise or word or inarticulate feeling that comes to you.

If the memory of the event with which you began should disappear and another memory—another painful emotion—should come to the surface, do not push it away. Let it come up. Let it bubble out.

This recipe often brings up the memory of forgotten events and feelings that accompany them. That is good. If they come to the surface, it is because you are ready to deal with them and wash them out of your system.

Continue to inhale through the nose out of the water, and exhale by bubbling with your entire face in the water, until you feel that you have worked off your painful memories. Create a full-blown storm in a tea cup.

When you are quite sure you have done enough, do one thing more. Take one more deep breath. This time, as you exhale, bubble out a word of liberation and serenity.

If you feel like crying, cry.

Or, if you find this whole procedure all too comic, laugh

Then say goodbye to that disagreeable event, to the un

pleasant feelings and words that you have bubbled out,
and empty the bowlful of them into the kitchen sink.

There are some variations on this recipe.

Instead of putting their feet in hot water and bubbling
through cold, some prefer to keep their feet in cold water
and bubble through hot.

Some do the recipe while sitting in a hot tub and holding the bowl of ice water between their hands.

Do whichever you find most agreeable. The principle is
the same.

*Note: For any recipe involving differences of temperature,
you may want to consult your doctor.*

Times when *Bubble Freedom* is especially beneficial
are:

After a day of dull and taxing work in a stuffy office.

Before going out to a party.

On a morning when you have some difficulty in beginning your day.

At night, if any insistent thought or worry keeps you
awake or restless.

When you feel a migraine, or some other form of headache or tension coming on, experiment with this recipe,
using various combinations of temperatures. There is a
good chance that it will dispel your tension without your
having to take any form of medication.

Besides developing beauty from within by erasing the
ugly feeling that mars beauty, this recipe is excellent for
the complexion and especially good for wrinkles, since it

stimulates the circulation of the blood through the facial tissues and gives the face a look of freshness. It is particularly effective for the lips and mouth. Remember to let your lips go free and loose under the water and make a lot of noise with your bubbling. A good storm in a tea cup will clear the air.

It works—if you work

There may be certain recipes for which you feel a marked aversion. If so, ask yourself why. Do this when you are not practicing the recipe. Be curious about the causes for this aversion.

15. GIVE SOMETHING FOR NOTHING

In 1940, when Italy rather suddenly entered World War II, I was a young Italian violinist concertizing in the United States.

It became almost impossible and certainly dangerous to cross the Atlantic. My father cabled me to remain in this country. He thought it was better to have his daughter far away, even for a long time, than take the chance of having her blown up by a misdirected torpedo.

My life was completely changed by this event. I was stranded in America, and after Pearl Harbor I was declared an enemy alien. But nothing in the behavior of my American friends and acquaintances ever gave the slightest impression that we were enemies. I could write a great deal about being an enemy alien in America. My world had been shattered, my career interrupted, yet, because of the generosity of my American friends, that period remains one of the indelibly beautiful experiences of my life.

I want to tell you about a trivial, yet for me very important, episode of that period. It was summer and I was in a small town in Arkansas. Everyone was wearing immaculately white shoes. I was the guest of friends and, never having been in an American home before, I did not have the slightest idea of the mechanics that make it run. How everybody kept their shoes so white was a mystery. In the evening I had put mine outside the door, as is customary in Europe, expecting to find them clean in the morning. Nothing happened. The shoes were just put back in my room.

I was very young and shy; most of my life had been spent playing the violin, and I was absurdly inexperienced in other matters.

In the meantime my shoes were getting dirtier and dirtier. How did people get their white shoes so clean? I had no idea. In my normal state I would simply have asked someone to explain the mystery. But my state was not normal—I was full of anxiety. I had had no news from my family and there were press reports that my native city had been bombed. When our spirits are low, so is our resourcefulness.

I was utterly depressed, and one afternoon, while talking about my situation to my friend, I burst into tears. "And now, on top of everything else, my white shoes are getting blacker and blacker!"

My friend, a sophisticated young woman, said nothing. A little later I found the white shoes in my room, whiter than when I bought them. I rushed to my friend to ask who had done the cleaning and how much should I tip or pay.

She laughed, "There is no one to pay—I did it." Then nonchalantly she added, "Didn't you know that I love to clean white shoes?"

It was at that moment that the essence of this recipe was revealed to me; now I pass it on to you.

Give Something for Nothing

It is impossible!

It is impossible to give something for nothing.

This is true regardless of how the person to whom we give responds to our giving. The simple act of setting out to give something for nothing already brings us a return. This is so, apart from morality, apart from duty. If I can give without any thought of return, it means that I can *afford* to give. I am made rich by the act of giving.

Most of our human relationships are exchanges, trades. We trade favors, kindnesses, attentions; we also trade unkindnesses, enmities, neglects. The human being is a reactive, responsive organism, and usually his response is of the same quality as the stimulus. The primitive savage within us tends to respond to violence with violence, to friendliness with friendliness.

In our complex world, our trades are not quite so simple. Most of our giving is to get something in return, although not necessarily of the same kind or from the same person. Often we calculate the return, realistically or not, as the case may be. Often we expect lifelong gratitude or special recognition for what we have given or done. And often we are disappointed and disillusioned. The return is nothing like what we have anticipated.

The answer to this riddle is simple: the giver measures his gift with one yardstick, and the receiver measures it with another. People differ in their values as they differ in their needs. It is as though you and I, living in two different countries, were to buy and sell land to each other, and you were to buy a kilometer of Mediterranean beach from me under the impression that it was an American mile. Imagine your resentment when you came to take possession, and found that I had sold you only a little more than half of what you thought you paid for.

When we buy and sell we are careful to know the measures; in land, goods, and money they are fairly exact; and, if we make a bad trade, we usually have only ourselves to blame.

But when we make other trades our measures are subjective. Only I know what my giving has cost me in time, trouble, or emotion. Only the recipient knows what my gift means to him.

What happens when your response is less than I thought I had the right to expect? I am angry or hurt; I feel I am a victim of your thoughtlessness, or the world's. I feel unrecognized, undervalued; I am pained and embittered. I say, "Look at all that I have given, and what do I get? Nothing."

This kind of giving is not giving, but trading. When we think of it as giving we are bound to suffer disappointment, and the painful, harmful feelings that go with disappointment.

The other kind of giving is for the giving itself. It has no strings attached, no expectations either open or concealed. The person who gives for the pleasure he gets out of giving is usually satisfied and happy with the act itself. The act of giving is its own reward. If something comes in return it is an unanticipated piece of good luck.

This recipe asks you to perform, voluntarily, consciously, the act of giving something for nothing. Here are the preparatory steps to giving something for nothing.

Recognize the difference between:

giving something with the conscious or unconscious expectation of being paid back, and

voluntarily giving something without expecting a return.

Ask yourself:

Have I in the past given something and received nothing? Did I feel cheated?

Was I giving in order to get, or was I genuinely giving something for nothing?

If I really intended to give something for nothing, why did I resent getting nothing in return?

Recognize your feelings as you set out voluntarily to give something for nothing.

Do you like yourself? Then like yourself.
Do you feel like a fool? Then feel like a fool.

Are you furious at this recipe? Or at its author? Then be furious.

Recognize that you are setting out to do the impossible. Go out and do it. Freely and voluntarily give something for nothing.

The choice is vast. Do not strain too much in trying to keep anonymity, or in trying to find someone who will not appreciate your giving. In other words, do not strain too much to get nothing out of giving—it is impossible. For you will get something, somehow, if not from others then from yourself. So, do not think too much; lightly and non-chalantly—

Give Something for Nothing

Here is a list of possibilities for the impossible task of trying to give something for nothing.

Bring a flower to someone who never receives any.

Ask someone's opinion about a subject he knows very well.

Take someone to the theater.

Anticipate another's need and take care of it.

Help an in-law, without strings.

Let your parent help you, in his way, not in yours.

Cook someone his favorite meal.

Let your child help you, in his way, not in yours.

Call up a lonely old person.

Give a specific thoughtful compliment.

Let someone talk to you for two hours. Never say the pronoun "I."

Clean someone's shoes.

Add to this list:

It works—if you work

It is by an evolutionary process of growing from within that we come to realize our native potentialities—not by a mechanical and servile conformity to some predetermined pattern. Look upon the recipes, not as set patterns, but as useful, versatile tools.

---

16. AS IF FOR THE FIRST TIME

or Five Minutes of Beauty a Day

This is a recipe for beauty—*for experiencing beauty.*

When you can do this recipe for even a few seconds, you will realize an extraordinary release and liberation. When you can make a practice of it, you will join a company of very advanced people. The more artificial, hurried, and graceless your life is, the more you will benefit from this recipe.

It is a recipe for pure enjoyment.

To do this recipe well and thoroughly will take no more than five minutes a day. Have you that much time for the experience of beauty?

Beauty starvation is almost as widespread as love starvation. Often we do not realize that this is what we are hungry for. In our world of traffic jams and artificial flowers we are so far removed from the pure experiences of our senses that we do not even realize our deprivation.

Sensory deprivation and the heightening of perception are the subjects of vast study of the part of scientists, psychologists, and artists. There is a close connection, yet a mysterious one, between our state of being and our perceptions. University courses, laboratory experiments, drugs, fasts, ancient religious practices—all these approaches are being used to study our perceptual responses to the outer world, and the ways in which our organism as a whole reacts to these responses. Volumes are being written on this fascinating research.

You and I are not theorizing here, but doing. My recipe does not ask you to fast, take drugs, or study for years. It does not involve you in laboratory experimentation. It asks only five minutes of daily attention to your perceptions, just as they are.

There is one thing it asks you *not* to do. It asks you not to think, not to describe, not to compare. It asks you not to be conscious at all of words. Drop them, lose them, leave them behind, and enter the world of pure sensation.

For this recipe, choose any kind of beauty you prefer, with the provision that it be a natural beauty. Choose a beauty outside yourself, not one which may be within you, in your memory or imagination. Choose to receive five minutes of beauty through any of your senses.

To begin with, give your attention to only one sense: taste only—touch only—see only—hear only. If more than one sensation makes its way to you, do not willfully keep it out of your consciousness, but do not give it your attention either: simply let it be. Fix your attention on the one sense you have chosen.

Here are the directions:

> Choose the kind of beauty you are going to communi‑ cate with today.
>
> Cancel all thoughts from your mind.
>
> Do not name or describe or classify.

Make no reference to other beauties of the past or future.

Simply receive beauty, as it is.

For example, choose a taste, the taste of an apple. Bite into the apple. Taste it, without thinking about any other apple bite you have ever experienced. Simply taste the *appleness* of that apple.

Or choose to experience beauty through your sense of smell: breathe the fragrance of a flower. Breathe it, without thinking whether it is the most fragrant, the sweetest, the best. Do not describe, compare, measure. Become absorbed in the fragrance.

Choose to see beauty. Watch a puppy's antics. Do not think of how he will look or behave when he is a grown dog. Look at him now, look at him fully, look at him so completely that there is no room in your mind for anything except this puppy, *this* moment.

Listen to the rain—only listen.
Listen to the wind—only listen.
Listen to the sea—only listen.

If you choose to feel beauty through touch, only touch. Do not move your hand; only leave your hand on what you are touching—and receive.

In doing this recipe:

Find a comfortable position.

Move as little as possible.

Remain still.

When you can do this recipe well, even for a few moments, you will experience a great sense of release from your familiar, everyday self.

This recipe is three thousand years old; it was given by Shiva to the goddess Parvati. Shiva said:

"Radiant one, see *as if for the first time* a beauteous person or an ordinary object."

As if for the first time—this is the essence.

It works—if you work

What is "normal"? Recapture a time in your life when you felt yourself at a peak, when your entire organism was strong and unified and vibrant: consider that time your normal. Keep that peak present in your mind as your true natural state.

17. AIR, WATER, FOOD

Love, joy, peace—the fruits of the spirit.

Air, water, food—the roots of the body.

If the roots are cut off, the tree will die. Less severe damage will not kill the tree, but its growth will be stunted and distorted, its capacity to bear fruit will be diminished. There will be little love, less joy and no peace.

The purpose of all the recipes is to clear the way for love, joy, and peace.

For this, we need a body that is functioning at its best. This functioning is sometimes disturbed by thoughts and emotions. At other times, it is disturbed by physical causes. One of the main physical causes is poor air, water, and food.

The subject of air, water and food is a sad subject nowadays. For we ourselves have polluted and poisoned these essentials of human life.

The air we breathe is contaminated with the fumes of automobiles and chimneys, and now with that most serious of all contaminations, the radioactive dust of nuclear fallout.

Our water is befouled by industrial and urban wastes.

Our food is tainted with the poisons of man-made chemicals in pesticides and insecticides, and the processes by which it is prepared for us often remove the very life-giving elements, the vitamins and minerals on which good health depends.

Today we are beginning to be aware of the harm we do to ourselves by tampering with the natural environment. More and more urgently scientists are warning us, and we are beginning to listen. The revelations by Rachel Carson in her book, *The Silent Spring*, have at last convinced many people of what organic farmers and health food followers have long known. That is, that our food has been even more seriously tampered with than has our air and water. The chemical poisons put into our plants and food and fed to our domestic animals will soon reach dangerous proportions if we do not insist that our government take steps to control the use of chemicals.

Meanwhile, we must breathe air, drink water, eat food. The way we use these three essentials is partly within our control. The complex problems of what we breathe, drink and eat are beyond the scope of these pages. This recipe is intended as a reminder that we can be fully well only if we give due attention to our body as well as our psyche.

Each one of us is benefited by a study of natural nutrition; and the materials for this study are available to all of us. In health food stores, book stores, and public libraries, there is a vast choice of good books and magazines on the subject of natural nutrition.

These books are occasionally contradictory; yet you will realize quickly that you need not become fanatic about one diet or another. Many diets good for specific purposes can be lacking in some vital nutrient. Rigidity is unwholesome in food as in anything else.

You will find that there are a few basic principles agreed upon by most authorities.

Here they are:

> *Choose, whenever possible, food that is organically grown. (There are many such markets in California, where this movement began, and they are spreading across the country.)*

> *Choose live food. Processed, refined, treated, canned or precooked food cannot be live.*

> *Choose food you enjoy.*

> *Cook your food with as little heat as possible. Overcooked foods are not live.*

> *Learn to read labels.*

Choosing a loaf of bread is a good example of the last principle.

How do you choose your bread?

I counted fifty-six different breads in a supermarket. Besides taste and price, what should one look for?

Be wary of any label with long, difficult words.

Foods are on store shelves for millions of men and women to buy and eat, not for a few chemistry professors to read and understand. If it has whole flour, water, honey, salt and yeast, a loaf needs little else to be good bread.

Favor foods generally which are labeled: "No preservatives" or "Nothing added."

Be wise about nutrition—but keep this wisdom in the kitchen.

We defeat ourselves when we serve a nutrition lecture with the food!

When you prepare a healthful dish, forget its nutritional advantages when you bring it to the table. Many people are bored or even repelled by the thought that the food they eat is "good for them."

Give your carefully prepared dish some glamor.

Say: "This recipe just came from Paris. I got it from Jacqueline—who got it from the chef at the Ritz—who made her swear never to give it to anyone! And she just arrived and gave it to me!"

How much more exciting that is than saying: "Here's a little something that will delay the onset of arteriosclerosis!"

Attitudes toward food are often determined by our experiences in childhood—whether we had too much or too little food, how it was presented.

"Eat liver—it is good for you."

"But I don't like it."

"Eat it anyway. It's good for you."

Eat fish; it is brain food. Eat spinach; it will make you strong. Eat parsnips. Never mind the taste, eat it because it is *good* for you. Good foods, and good-tasting foods, are rejected forever because they bear the parent's label, "it's good for you!"

If you want your children to avoid such attitudes toward food, to keep an open mind about foods, take a hint from an intelligent mother. This is the way she introduces her young child to a new food:

She never mentions the names of foods.

She says: "Eat this. Taste that

If the child says, "I don't like it," she answers, "You

don't like it *today*. Tomorrow or next week, you can decide again. It will be different next time anyway because it will not be the same piece of food. It will come from a different tree or a different garden or a different farm."

Thus, for the child, the food does not have a label. He reacts to the taste of food, not to its name.

It is a wise old rule that grownups at the table should not make remarks about food in front of children. Children automatically react to adult remarks and tend to imitate adult attitudes toward food.

The less said about food the better—especially while eating it.

Query: Might there not be fewer quarrels and better digestion if the first ten or fifteen minutes of a family meal were pleasantly silent? Try it!

We eat because we are hungry—but also for a number of other reasons. Next time you are invited to a restaurant ask yourself the following questions:

How do I make my choice of foods and drinks?

To satisfy my desire?

To please my host?

To fulfill my nutritional requirement?

Because a gourmet would choose it?

To try something new?

Because it is expensive?

Because it is cheap?

To show my sophistication?

To hide my lack of sophistication?

To impress the head waiter?

Because I am hungry?

Food is often connected with emotion, and it is no wonder. When we were children, food, attention and love were usually given to us by the same person. Many psychological hungers transform themselves into physical hungers. We eat out of loneliness, anxiety, boredom. That is why the problem of overweight is so complex.

The unequal distribution of food is one of the world's most tragic facts. Millions of people die because they have too little to eat, and many die because they have too much. Heart disease and a number of other physical and psychological ills are related to excess weight.

In most cases mental illness springs from emotional, psychological, or genetic causes. It may also be due to nutritional deficiencies. Actual personality changes may accompany thyroid deficiency, which is generally due to a shortage of iodine. The same is true of pellagra, which results from a shortage of vitamin B complex. Other nutritional shortages also cause grave psychological and emotional disturbances.

In an article in the *Journal of Psychology,* entitled "Is Mental Illness Mental?" Dr. G. Watson lists the following disorders as caused by faulty nutrition: ideas of persecution, mental confusion, loss of memory, depression, disorderly thinking, anxiety. All of these and other strictly psychological states were corrected by nutritional means only.

Even more interesting is the fact that these conditions were induced in psychologically normal volunteers entirely by experimental diets which were deficient in certain specific elements.

Revealing studies have been made in the question of blood sugar, as Dr. E. M. Abrahamson, M.D., tells us in his interesting book, *Body, Mind and Sugar.* Not only low

energy and low spirits but even delinquency and alcohol-
ism have been connected with low blood sugar which may
result from dependence upon cola drinks, candy bars and
other unnutritious substitutes for sound and nourishing
food.

Often people who have come to me to discuss their
problems have told me that they are taking tranquilizers.

I ask them when they take the tranquilizers.

Frequently the answer is that they take them three hours,
more or less, after eating, a time when the blood sugar
is very low and when nervousness, tension, anger and
especially indecision tend to be very high.

What mind and body need then is not tranquilization
but fuel—good, natural fuel—to fortify the blood and re-
plenish the energy sources of the cells.

I have suggested that these people eat wholesome, high-
energy food such as a bit of cheese and fruit which together make an excellent restorer of energy, or a banana
or a handful of almonds and raisins.

In many cases, the tranquilizers have been forgotten
because they were no longer needed.

When you are driving back and forth to work or school,
going out with the children, going to the office or to the
country or anywhere at all, keep a box of good things to
nibble in the car, dried fruits such as figs, dates, prunes,
almonds and pignolas and other nuts. Not only are these
ideal nourishment, full of essential food elements, but
they also give immediate energy, so important in the tense
struggle with traffic. Instead of arriving at your destination
frantic for a stimulant, or depending upon coffee shops
along the road with their unsatisfying pies and ice cream,
you can keep the driver's and the passengers' energies and

spirits up with the little pantry in the dashboard compartment.

The first cell was born in water. We all spend our first nine months of life before birth in a gentle, cushioning bed of water. After millions of years of evolution, the human body's weight is about seventy percent water. The water in our bodies, scientists believe, still contains the same percentage of salt as the ancient sea in which life was born almost three billion years ago.

The use of water to cure illness is far older than any drug. The wonderful book of hydrotherapy by Father Sebastin Kneipp has gone through fifty editions in eight years and is still in print.* Father Kneipp's methods have brought relief to thousands of people suffering from a variety of ills.

In some of these recipes we use water, sometimes in actuality, sometimes in imagination. Water is soothing to the skin, relaxing to the muscles, the nerves, the mind; swimming has been called the perfect exercise. Water is beautiful to the eyes and the ears; listen to a river, to the ocean.

Sit near a fountain whenever you can. Better still, have a fountain of your own. Now there are little home fountains to be bought for a few dollars. The water spurting up and falling again in little drops creates negative ions.

What are negative ions? We have heard so much about them lately, since it was discovered that they are crucial to our well-being and that they are lost through air pollution. Ions are simply electrically charged particles, either positive or negative, and they are a natural part of our air. Usually they are in balance, but when this balance is

* *My Water Cure*, Health Research, Lafayette St., Mokelumne Hill, Cal.

disturbed, as it is by pollutants, or a falling barometer, there is an excess of positive ions in the air and we feel stuffy, dull, irritable.

Negative ions are stimulating and energizing. Some scientists believe that negative ions can ease pain. Many people have small electrical ionizers in their homes or offices, or ionizing attachments on their air conditioners.

Water breaking in droplets releases negative ions into the air. That is why we feel exhilarated at the seashore or beside a waterfall. The ancient Persians, the Arabs and the Moors in Spain always had a fountain in their gardens —they had never heard about negative ions, but they knew that a fountain was refreshing. You can have your own little fountain; it uses the same small quantity of water automatically springing up and returning, spraying the air you breathe with refreshing, energizing negative ions.

Did you breathe today?

Ask yourself that question. Ask a friend. Begin by saying, "This question requires a yes or no answer. When I ask it, don't think. Just answer quickly with the first thing that comes to your mind." Then ask quickly, "Did you breathe today?"

The number who answer "no" will surprise you.

Your own answer to that question may surprise you.

Breathing can be either conscious or unconscious. It is one of the few vital functions that we ourselves can direct —how often we forget that astonishing fact!

A conscious and knowing control of breathing can solve many psycho-physical problems. The Yoga teaching is divided into many branches, but all of them make use of the art of breathing of which the Yogi are the greatest masters.

Even a limited study of this principle has a vastly beneficial influence in our life.

Many of the recipes in this book ask you to be conscious of your breathing, or to use your breathing in certain ways. On page 33 there are some general directions for breathing. Here are some special hints in the use of breathing for particular situations:

> When you are in a state of tension, anger or distress of any kind, stop for a moment. Put aside, for this moment, every concern, every thought. Take three long, deep breaths. Make them perfect breaths. Begin each one, as in the directions on page 33, by exhaling completely; breathe out, out, out, every bit of air in your lungs. Then, and then only, inhale: inhale long and deeply through the nose. Fill yourself completely—and hold the breath. Again, breathe out, out, out. Take three such breaths. Now go back to the situation you must deal with, and you will find yourself much better able to deal with it.

> When you are kept waiting, especially when what you are waiting for is unpleasant and makes you anxious or tense: clear your mind of the thought of waiting and what you are waiting for, and for several minutes attend only to the way you breathe. Think of nothing else; simply follow your breathing. Observe consciously how you take in the air, how you hold it, how you expel it. Observe particularly the instants between those three actions, those fractions of a second when there is no inhaling, no holding of the breath, no exhaling.

> When you want to reduce your smoking: each time you are about to light a cigarette, pause first, and take five long, slow breaths, concentrating only on them.

> At any time, whether or not you are consciously tired, nervous, or tense, refresh yourself in this way: make

yourself yawn by taking a few deep breaths and stretching. Yawning is the body's own reflex way of refreshing its tired cells by oxygenating the blood and accelerating the circulation. Incidentally it is excellent for the complexion because it especially brings circulation to the face.

The voice is a telltale sign of the psycho-physical state. How often have you observed that your husband or wife, your child or your friend is tense, anxious, depressed—or happy and full of good news—simply by the quality of the voice you hear! The voice is produced by the breath. That is why singing lessons would be good for all of us, regardless of talent or ambition. They would make us conscious of our breathing and teach us to breathe well. Remember to give support to your voice with good breathing; not only your voice but your whole person, body and mind, mood and emotions, will benefit.

Find your *real* voice.

The way we breathe affects our state of mind; this is simple fact. Good breathing habits make for good thinking and feeling; bad breathing habits for poor thinking and unsatisfactory feeling.

Proper *respir*ation is one of the conditions of high *aspira*tion and creative *inspir*ation.

It works—if you work

Life will always present problems. Recipes do not elim-inate them: they help you to change your reaction and your attitude toward these problems and thus put you in a better position to understand and solve them.

18. *THROW WORDS AWAY*

Imagine that you are very thirsty. Imagine that you are crossing a desert and you are desperately thirsty. You would give anything for a cup of water. Indeed, you would give your life, for you will soon lose it anyway if you do not have that cup of water.

Say the word "water" aloud. Write it in the sand. See it before your eyes: W-A-T-E-R.

Will those letters quench your thirst? Will the repetition of the sound save you from dying for lack of water? Of course not.

The word "water" is an arbitrary sign. So are the sounds we make when we say it, and the symbols with which we write it. The fluid that quenches our thirst, and on which our life literally depends, is another matter, totally different from W-A-T-E-R.

Now suppose again that you are in the desert, dying of thirst. Suddenly, something cool and wet begins to drip on your skin, to glide down your parched throat. The cool moisture is not "water," the word; it is neither sign nor symbol. It is the mystery of immediate experience, the *thing* to which the word "water" refers.

Words are man's invention—a most wonderful but also a most dangerous invention. Thanks to words, we can behave like human beings, sometimes like angels. But also, thanks to words, we can behave as malignantly as devils and more stupidly than the dumb beasts.

Our emotions are ever-changing and infinitely varied, but the words with which we describe them are fixed and rigid. Our life is like quicksilver, our vocabulary like steel. Sometimes a consummate poet succeeds in rendering the quality of life in words. For the rest of us, this is not possible.

The influence of words on our emotional behavior has been recognized in many civilizations.

Dorothy Lee, the anthropologist who made a study of the Oglala Indians in this country, tells us that their children were brought up *first* in relatedness to life—*and then* in relatedness to words. She writes:

"The mother initiated her newborn baby into relatedness with nature and continued to do so in various ways through his infancy. She took the very young baby out and merely pointed to natural manifestations without labeling. Only after the baby experienced directly, only later, did she offer him concepts." *

It is of great value for us to find the interrelation of words and experience. It is surprising how much our emotions are involved in an artificial agglomeration of consonants and vowels.

Are you not convinced?

Prove it to yourself by a small, if somewhat uncomfortable, experiment. Abstain from liquids, including fruits and vegetables, which are mainly liquid, long enough to

* *New Knowledge in Human Values*, A. H. Maslow, ed. Harper, 1959.

be deeply, genuinely thirsty—thirsty enough to understand a man marooned in the desert. Then, when you are
desperately thirsty, you will probably be able to experience water, the element, without the word W-A-T-E-R.

If you do not want to do this experiment, simply wait
until a time when you are very thirsty. Abstain from water
a little longer. Repeat the word "water" and see if it
quenches your thirst.

The following recipe is not as realistic as dying of thirst
in the desert, but it is revealing and rewarding.

> Make a list of the words which are for you the most
> sacred and the most profane—a list of words that give
> you strong reactions. Does one of these words make
> you blush? make you cry? make you angry? give you
> indigestion? give you a stiff neck?—

Here is a list of words, each of which may carry a strong
emotional charge for most of us:

God	Daddy	sin
ugly	father	dirty
brother	teacher	fool
sister	go away	crazy
sex	not now	jerk
shut up	hopeless	bum
baby	hopeful	none of your business
hellfire	joy	bitch
minister	impossible	slut
church	earth	obedient
doctor	peace	disobey
bad	money	tramp
good	selfish	coward
mother	never	yellow
Mommy	always	

Now, add your own charged words or phrases (next
page).

Choose a word which for you is heavily charged with power or emotion.

Repeat that word, again and again, until an emotion, possibly a memory, or other words or ideas emerge in you. It is good if memories, ideas, and pictures emerge. Do not stop them. But, in this recipe, follow mainly the emotion.

Let the emotion take over completely. If the word or words are swallowed by the emotion, let them be swallowed. Let the emotion reach its climax.

When it is at its climax, let it become—make it become —an action. It can be an action as violent as breaking a stone or as gentle as caressing a cat with a peacock's feather. It may be an action as useful as mowing the lawn, or as non-utilitarian as desperate sobbing; it may be painting with your fingers, doing a wild dance, or waxing the kitchen floor.

Do not label your emotion and action. Feel and do without naming.

Repeat this procedure with the same word until that word has become a useful tool, not a controlling dictator.

It works—if you work

Some suffering is unavoidable; some, on the contrary, is strictly man-made. We bring it on ourselves. The recipes will help you to avoid the suffering that is unnecessary, to use and transform the suffering that cannot be avoided. Use your problems; use your suffering. Do not let them use you.

19. DON'T THROW WORDS AROUND

Throw words away, as we have said in the previous recipe. But do not throw them around.

Words are powerful and must be handled with care. Under certain circumstances and for certain people a casual word may strike with the force of a dangerous missile. Words can penetrate the vulnerable mind like barbed arrows. Having penetrated, they can be extracted only with the greatest difficulty.

The chief victims of these unintentional barbs are all people who are sick or laboring under physical or mental stress, all people who are semiconscious, unconscious or sleeping, and children in particular.

Children are more suggestible than grownups and much more literal-minded. I knew a small girl who heard that the neighbors had fired their cook; for weeks afterward she lived in a state of horrified shock: those apparently nice people across the road had set their poor cook on fire!

A friend of mine remembered from his childhood that when he went on an errand to the grocery store, his mother warned him about a dangerous crossing: "Be sure to look up and down." Being a very obedient boy, when he

reached the curb he faithfully looked up—at the sky—
and then down—at the earth; then out of a natural sense
of self-preservation he also looked to left and right along
the street. He told me:

"On occasion I would omit the sky and earth look, and
then I felt like a very bad boy. Years after we moved away,
it suddenly dawned on me what my mother meant—that
I must look in both directions up and down the street. If
I had been merely obedient I could have been killed."

A child will often accept quite literally some casual over-
heard remark about himself. A tired, anxious mother may
say in Johnny's hearing, "Johnny is always sick." If the boy
is lucky, nothing will come of it. But sometimes the fearful
or ambiguous words may "take" like an inoculation, and
force a pattern of some recurrent psychosomatic illness
upon his organism.

Even more powerful are ambiguous or negative words
spoken by an adult to a child who is confused or frightened.
A woman of about thirty-five came to me complaining that
she was always being accused of lying. "You are the only
one who knows whether the accusation is true," I said. She
answered that she was not quite sure. The only thing she
was certain of was that at times she did lie, but she had no
idea why she did. Usually the lie would not benefit her in
any way, and she knew she would be found out.

We pursued the matter further. She recounted and in
fact relived a most painful experience when she was eight
years old. Her father had unjustly accused her of lying and
ordered her to confess. When she protested her innocence
he became furious; while spanking her with a strap he
shouted repeatedly, "I'll teach you to be a liar, I'll teach
you to be a liar!"

He certainly did. This grown woman was still acting in obedience to that command, given to her while she was in a state of physical pain, confusion and fear, and given, furthermore, by that powerful, punishing giant, her father. She grew to hate her father, and this hatred only added the negative energy of guilt to the compulsion to lie, which had endured through all those twenty-seven years.

Similar accidents with words can happen to adults as well. On the conscious level we are relatively rational, but on the subconscious level we remain as literal-minded and as suggestible as we were in childhood. In sickness, under strong negative emotion, in physical or mental stress or on the borderline of consciousness—in any of these states our conscious mind is partly shut down and our subconscious mind accepts and records whatever is said within earshot.

From the time of Hippocrates, every good doctor has understood the therapeutic value of confidence and hope, has known how dangerous it is for the sick to hear the wrong kind of words. And the wrong kind of words may be uttered with the best intentions.

Here, for example, is a woman about to undergo surgery. The surgery is not serious, but the patient is apprehensive, and drowsy from sedatives. A well-meaning comforter reassures her: "Don't worry, dear—it will all be over in less than two hours."

What can be wrong with that? For the conscious mind it would probably be reassuring. But the conscious mind is not quite there; illness and anxiety have left the field open to the subconscious mind, and this takes whatever is said with the utmost literalness. "It will all be over in less than two hours!" So far as the subconscious mind is concerned, it means that in less than two hours it will be all over with her—she will be dead! All over . . . all over . . . it is with this dismal and debilitating thought that she goes to the operating room.

Fortunately this woman expressed her fear to the anesthetist, who immediately understood and counteracted it with careful and comforting reassurance.

All good anesthetists are aware nowadays of the power of words on anxious, semiconscious and even on completely unconscious patients. It is now generally accepted that the perception of sound persists long after the perception of pain has been anesthetized. This is interestingly explained by Dr. Milton J. Marmer, chief anesthesiologist of the Cedars of Lebanon Hospital in Los Angeles, in his book, *Hypnosis in Anesthesiology*. Surgery is a special case of mental and physical stress. To a lesser degree the same principle holds in other stressful situations such as painful emotions, exhaustion, sickness and shock.

Consider the words or phrases that you habitually say in certain situations; examine their many meanings; experience the impact of these meanings on yourself; "jump into the other's place."

For instance:

> *To a child, husband, wife, with whom one is annoyed: "That's just what I might have expected of you."*

> *To a person who has just had a mishap, failure, defeat of some kind: "That's you all over; always the fall guy! Sucker! You ALWAYS have bad luck!*

> *"You always forget your lessons!"*

> *"You can't remember anything!"*

> *"You MUST BE accident prone!"*

Now examine the many meanings of those words—experience their impact on yourself—"jump into the other's place."

The directions for this recipe are of the simplest:

Do not use any of these phrases if you are IN THE PRESENCE OF INJURED, SICK, UPSET, UNCONSCIOUS, OR SLEEPING PERSONS OF ANY AGE. Keep Silent.

Silence is wonderful, especially when you are with a person with whom you have good understanding and communication. However, there are people for whom silence has alarming associations. Then it is good to soothe and reassure. Children and adults in trouble want to know that someone cares, and that they have help nearby. Sometimes words are very good indeed. Speak, then, very little and clearly, and choose words that are completely unequivocal.

The best thing is just to ask, "What happened?"

But let me warn you: you may receive an answer full of anger. This anger is not directed at you—you are not the target. (This is yet another occasion to keep that recipe well in mind and in the muscles.) Let the person tell you everything he wants to. Do not comment; simply listen.

If asking what happened does not meet the situation, if it is best for the person to remain quiet, then reassure him with words or phrases that cannot possibly be misinterpreted, like one of those on the opposite page:

"Everything is going to be all right."
"You can take care of it."
"It is not going to happen again."
"We can fix it."
"It is not as bad as it seems."
"It is not serious."
"It will pass."

It works—if you work

It is good to do more than one recipe within the same period of time. The recipes are profoundly different from each other, as contradictory as our own moods, desires, and needs. One says "float and do nothing," and another, "do something immeditaely"; one says "be completely yourself," and the next "jump into the other's place." When you do more than one recipe you are clearing more than one facet of yourself.

20. SONG WITHOUT WORDS

Words are good servants but bad masters. Many of us have become the slaves of words, and we are not even aware of their tyranny. We do as words tell us to do. We become what they tell us to be. We feel what they tell us to feel, and as often as not they are not even our words, but other people's words.

We attach words to everything, and indiscriminately. We attach the word *love* to our feelings for the beloved or for a dress, a drink, God, our new convertible. It is rare and difficult for us to see a beautiful sunset without telling ourselves or others how beautiful it is.

Besides the words and noises of our personal lives, we are continuously hammered by words and noises typical of our modern world. As Aldous wrote, in *Perennial Philosophy,*

"The twentieth century is, among other things, the Age of Noise. Physical noise, mental noise and noise of desire —we hold history's record for all of them. And no wonder: for all the resources of our almost miraculous technology have been thrown into the current assault against silence. The most popular and influential of all recent inventions, the radio [and, since he wrote this, television] is nothing but a conduit through which prefabricated din can flow into our homes. And this din goes far deeper, of course, than the ear drums. It penetrates the mind, filling it with a babel of distractions—news items, mutually irrelevant bits of information, blasts of Corybantic or sentimental music, continually repeated doses of drama that bring no catharsis but merely create a craving for daily or even hourly emotional enemas. And where, as in most countries, the broadcasting stations support themselves by selling time to advertisers, the noise is carried from the ears, through the realms of phantasy, knowledge and feeling to the ego's central core of wish and desire."

This is a recipe for freeing the "ego's central core" from the tyranny of words and descriptive labels. A label is a device for classifying experiences, for putting things in pigeon holes. But in the real world pigeon holes do not exist—even the pigeons spend most of their time flying around.

This is a recipe for rediscovering the wonder of immediate experience, immediate feelings, immediate sensation, without the mediation of words. Bite, taste, caress, kiss, listen, see, feel, know—do these things in interior silence.

Interior silence is silence without words. For silence, too, can be noisy with unspoken words. Our so-called silences are usually filled with names, numbers, dates, places, things we must remember, things we want to do, the word labels for what we see, hear, feel, wish, believe. We play and replay recordings of past dialogues and of imaginary future ones.

Interior silence can help you to achieve rest. It can enrich pleasure. It can soften pain.

To achieve interior silence requires some practice.
Here is the method:

> Go to a place where you will be alone and undisturbed.
> Make yourself comfortable, sitting or lying down.
>
> Feel whatever is in you at the moment. If you wish, feel
> whatever feeling has lately been troubling you.
>
> Do not give a name to this feeling. Attach no words
> to it.
>
> Let the feeling fill you completely. Let it spread through
> all your being. Yet, observe it as if you were a bystander.
>
> Sitting or lying down, inwardly still, let feeling flow
> through you like a stream of silence, a song without
> words.
>
> If memories should emerge—faces, places, past events—
> don't interfere. Neither push them away, nor plunge
> into them. Only watch, and let them flow by.

The feeling you experience cannot be named. There are
no words for it, nor will you try to find words. Watch the
feeling, as you would watch a kitten playing, darting, leaping, tumbling. But not all our moods are playful. Sometimes when we look into ourselves we see something that
looks more like an angry bull. Then look at that bull. Observe its violence, power, brutality, its magnificence, its
misery.

You are the spectator. You are watching the feeling,
gentle or violent, good or bad, beautiful or ugly, as though
it were not your own, as though it were "out there" and
not "in here." You are watching it flow through you and
past you.

The quality or intensity of this feeling is of no importance.

You make no judgment of it, form no opinion.

You do not compare it or weigh it, approve or disapprove it.

You sit in solitude and allow the unnamed feeling to be itself, until, inevitably, it changes into something else, or dissolves.

When you become proficient in this recipe you will find it helpful in dealing with pain. Experiment with a small pain in this way:

> *Acknowledge the pain. It is there.*
>
> *But realize: you are not the pain.*
>
> *Do not deny its existence. But knowing that it is not you, watch it, observe it, follow its variations;*
>
> *Separate yourself from it, see it as a spectator.*
>
> *Say to yourself, "There is a pain. I am not the pain." (For more on this method of dealing with pain, see the recipe "Prajna NOW.")*

In the moment that you divide yourself from the pain, you are on the way to relief. It is also likely that you will fall into a healing, liberating sleep.

It works—if you work

Honesty with yourself is the essential condition for successfully practicing these recipes. Do them with all the honesty you can command. The first step is to recognize that you are not a static entity, but a living, dynamic creature, capable of self-discovery and change.

21. TLA-TLA-TLA

No, it is not the Tibetan Lamas Association; it is not the Trans-Lunar Airlines. It is something more immediate and useful to you, and it is available to you all the time.

T-L-A stands for "Talking-Listening-Acting."

> T—we talk to ourselves.
> L—we listen to what we say to ourselves.
> A—we act according to what we say.

TLA is one of our most powerful functions. So far as we know, it is exclusively human. Animals listen to and follow their senses and their instincts. Domesticated and trained, they also follow our commands. They listen to and obey their body needs, while we, all too often, ignore this direct information of body and instinct. Instead we listen to and follow our own internal dictates, rational or not.

Our TLA goes on automatically. Often unconsciously and sometimes disastrously. We are nearly always talking, for when we are not talking aloud we are usually talking within ourselves. We are our own best audience; we never interrupt. Even when we are asleep, there is some evidence that part of ourselves is still talking, and part is still listening. We are our own captive audience, twenty-four hours a day.

Our TLA is also used by others, and we also act on their suggestions. Modern merchandising makes cunning use of this human susceptibility with the immense semicaptive audience of radio and television.

TLA has made us receptive to great evil. Hitler showed us how the manipulation of minds—achieved through repetition of rhythmical slogans—could lead to wholesale slaughter. In his novel *Island* * Aldous Huxley probed the possibility of this power being used for the benefit of the human race.

A limpid and heart-shaking example of the paramount importance of TLA is a woman who for the first seven years of her life was deprived of it—Helen Keller. Until the age of seven the blind and deaf girl had no way to know that words existed, much less that one could speak them, hear them, see them—and she was like a violent, lost, wild animal in solitary confinement. The only communication with the world was through touch and taste. Then an extraordinary event happened:

"We [Helen and her teacher Anne Sullivan] walked down the path to the well house attracted by the fragrance of the honeysuckle with which it was covered. Someone was drawing water and my teacher placed my hand under the spout. As the cool stream gushed over one hand, she spelled into the other the word "water," first slowly, then rapidly. I stood still, my whole attention fixed upon the motion of her fingers. Suddenly I felt a mystic consciousness as of something forgotten, a thrill of returning thought, and somehow the mystery of language was re-

* Harper and Row, 1962.

vealed to me. I knew then that w-a-t-e-r meant the wonderfully cool something that was flowing over my hand. That living word awakened my soul, gave it light, hope, joy, set it free." *

Unlike Helen Keller, the overwhelming majority of children come into life with the innate capacity to learn and understand language. We use language in many ways: to organize our experience in a rational way; to communicate with other people; and to talk to ourselves—in other words —to make use of our TLA function. Man is a many sided organism with vast and varied potentials, many of which are never realized. We have in our power to choose which of our potentials we would like to develop to a maximum, and which we would prefer to minimize. Our TLA is an effective means of doing this.

By using TLA wisely we can also change external situations—for situations are almost always involved with *our* feelings, words, actions, which can be directly influenced by TLA. We must first recognize the power of TLA—then decide to use IT instead of being used BY it.

For instance, let us suppose I am often tired. There is not much sense in telling myself that I feel fresh and vigorous, when it is obviously untrue. But if I say: "I am always tired," with these words I make solid and stable a state of being which is likely to be only transitory. How much better to use my talking-listening-acting power not to confirm but to alleviate my fatigue. Instead of "I am always tired," I might say, "I can rest completely."

Another example: There are individuals—perhaps you know one—who through various circumstances have become convinced that people do not like them. Such an in-

* Helen Keller, *The Story of My Life.* Doubleday, 1954.

dividual may in fact be a difficult person to like. He tells himself, "Nobody likes me!" His attitude toward any new acquaintance is defensive, bristly, as though he were saying, "You are not going to like me anyway so I may as well give you good cause for your dislike!" Thus he feeds that aspect of his personality which makes him difficult to like, and thus he goes on saying to himself, "Nobody likes me." If such a person were to look more realistically into the situation he would find that it is he who prepares the ground —particularly his own interior ground—for people not to like him. And if he changed HIS attitude towards people, many of them would change THEIR attitude towards him. Thus an honest look would show him that his present lonely situation is to a great extent due to his destructive TLA-TLA-TLA.

This recipe proposes to substitute good-sense talk for non-sense talk. We are constantly changing, and it is in our power to influence, to direct, that change. Some facts of our lives are unchangeable, but we can change our attitude towards them. TLA-TLA-TLA is always there, ready to work for us or against us.

If one talks too much nonsense to oneself for too long a time, this nonsense will almost always "take." By stopping self-destructive repetition and making a fair appraisal of a situation, one can arrive at a more constructive, more creative way of directing oneself without distorting the truth.

Our aims in this recipe are twofold:

To end the automatic pattern of repeating to ourselves words and phrases that confirm and reinforce destructive or negative attitudes

To recognize that the immediate reality is not static, but fluid and changeable.

The directions have some points in common with self-improvement systems, past and present. They differ, as far as I know, in these ways:

> In this recipe not only words are used, but also music, rhythm, and—of paramount importance—our muscles.

> In these directions you are urged not to deny immediate reality.

Let us take an extreme example: I hate a person, and I say I love this person. This brings about an appalling conflict within me. Just imagine what would happen to your car if at the same time you were to use all its acceleration and all its brakes. This would probably wreck the car; it does not wreck us completely, perhaps, but it surely deprives us of strength to conquer the ugly emotion. It is not a spiritual achievement to say that I love when I hate, but it is a spiritual achievement to admit this feeling and say, "I am doing all I can to replace hate with understanding and consideration." It is a spiritual achievement not to judge the hated one. It is a spiritual achievement not to harm the hated one with actions, thoughts, or words. And of course it is a spiritual achievement to do some good to the hated person; this might dissolve the hate automatically.

In doing this recipe we must take care not to fool ourselves. People who have achieved a harmonious state of being are perhaps not so much more endowed than the rest of us with intelligence, character, or talent; they simply *fool themselves less.*

Whatever you want to improve, whether it is your health, your ability to get along with people, your memory or your golf stroke, the method is the same: you will still be using your TLA.

Here are the directions:

> *Make a list of traits or behavior patterns or functions which you wish to change. These changes may include almost everything except those facts which are unchangeable. Obviously, if you have brown eyes and would like them blue, no amount of TLA-TLA-TLA will make them blue. But you can change your attitude toward your brown eyes and be grateful for them.*

> *Choose one change at a time. Stay with it until you have achieved it. Then choose another. Do not try to make two changes at the same time.*

> *Put your wished-for attainment into a phrase.*
> *Say only what you know is possible.*
> *Say it in the present, not the future tense.*

With our TLA-TLA-TLA we are influencing our unconscious mind, which does not reason, criticize, choose, but only obeys in a literal way. If, for instance, you say, "Beginning tomorrow I will stop such-and-such a habit," this will always remain in the future. This is what happens with so many good proposals—they always begin tomorrow! But if you say, "Here and now I decide to . . ." this gives a direction effective *now*.

The impetus starts from the conscious, goes to the unconscious, comes back to the conscious in a constant merry-go-round; constructive or destructive according to your choice. When making up a phrase it is sometimes good to think of how you would talk to a child. Let us suppose you want to correct timidity in yourself: what is the most persuasive, logical, affirmative phrase you could say to free a child of *his* timidity? Use that phrase for yourself. Use words out of *your* everyday vocabulary. Make a short, clear phrase which feels natural to you and is easy to remember.

In using TLA-TLA-TLA we can address ourselves as "you," "I," with our first name, or indirectly by putting the emphasis on the action by using "it." For example: "It is getting better."

(*To explain:* In the early years of childhood we often refer to ourselves not as "I," but in the third person—"Mary wants candy"—and this childhood habit continues unconsciously with many of us in the adult life. When we use our TLA-TLA-TLA consciously we must take into account the possibility that we may still identify ourselves by the name that was used for us in childhood, perhaps a pet name or nickname.)

When you have chosen your phrase:

> *Choose a rhythmical tune. Combine that tune in rhythm with the words of your phrase.*
>
> *Sing the phrase, aloud if you are alone, silently if you are not.*
>
> *Sing the phrase in time with your movements as you perform a muscular exercise like tightening your stomach muscles, or when you are walking, jumping rope, beating eggs, rowing, punching or squeezing a ball, or with any action which can be rhythmically performed.*
>
> *Repeat the phrase with the music, mentally or silently. Repeat it, not only as words but also as body movements with the chosen rhythm. Tighten flabby muscles while you rhythmically repeat your phrase.*
>
> *Repeat the same phrase while resting and relaxing during the daytime, and—most important—repeat it until you*

go to sleep at night. When resting and relaxing or going to sleep do not sing the phrase, but only repeat it silently or in a low voice in an even, monotonous, expressionless murmur until you go to sleep.

The period between wakefulness and sleep is an important time to use our talking-listening-acting faculty. We are still in touch with our conscious mind and, at the same time, we are in communication with part of our subconscious mind. This part of our mind does not criticize or select, but is open to receive and follow suggestion. It is neutral, like a tape. You can record anything on that part of your mind—therefore what you record should be *clear, direct, constructive, and not liable to misinterpretation.*

Sing the phrase the moment you wake up in the morning and while you dress. Sing it as you prepare to go out to work, shop, on a date, or for an appointment.

By repeating this phrase in different forms and at different times we reach our organism at different levels:

When we rhythmically synchronize our words and our muscles we influence our physical self.

When we speak and listen to ourselves in a relaxed state we reach that level of our being where daydreaming takes place.

When we speak to ourselves on the borderline of sleep we reach the deeper level of our mind and give it direction.

This combined approach is very powerful. It is just as effective when it is used badly as when it is used well.

> It is important to speak to ourselves in a clear, unmistakable, constructive way, and never tell ourselves things which are ambiguous or NOT TRUE.
>
> When your mind begins a merry-go-round of destructive silent TLA-TLA-TLA, quickly replace it with your chosen phrase.
>
> When possible take a few slow, deep breaths before beginning the repetition of your phrase.

This is important: first of all when you breathe in the way described on page 33 you concentrate on the breathing, and the unconscious TLA-TLA-TLA automatically stops. Secondly, the method of breathing puts your body-mind in a receptive state, and thus your directions will be much more effective.

Some find it helpful to write their phrase on a piece of paper and attach it to the wrist with a rubber band while sleeping. This advice is given by Dr. Rolf Alexander in his excellent book, *Creative Realism*, where the subject of this recipe is fully developed.

Here are some sample phrases to help you phrase your own:

> It is getting easier to make decisions.
> It is getting more pleasant to meet new people.
> Stop nonsense talking *now*.
> Change is possible.
> This is changing.
> I can change.
> Change (your attitude) *now*.
> Here and now I decide to . . .
> Stop *now*.

Start *now*.

You don't need this (cigarette, drink, candy, etc.).

——— (your given name) can do it.

Our TLA-TLA-TLA is powerful, but it is not a cure-all. Use this recipe in conjunction with other recipes to achieve completeness.

Note: If you wish to see how effective this method is, try it with your child. Everything works more quickly with a child. In a short time you will see the effect.

Here is the method:

As you put your child to bed, give him a phrase to repeat. One that is used by an intelligent and loving mother I know is this: "It is fun to be good and happy and make everyone happy."

There is no need to explain or discuss the recipe or its purpose with the child; be especially careful to avoid talking about it in his hearing. It is merely another pleasant game you play as he prepares for bed, and again as he is dressing in the morning. You begin by saying it with him; presently he will be saying it by himself. Even if he is not yet speaking very well, let him say it; the younger, the better. Spend a few minutes with your child at bedtime, playing quietly and drowsily the game of being good and happy and making others happy; play the same game in a lively way when he gets up.

TLA-TLA-TLA is most powerful when we are children. Be aware *how* you use it when around them.

It works—if you work

Do not think of the recipes as being either for your mind or for your body. They are for you, one and undivided.

22. BE AN ANIMAL

Go into a room where you can be alone and undisturbed for half an hour or longer.

Take some simple food with you, fruit or bread, but no knife, fork, or spoon.

Throw off all your clothes. And—

Be an animal

You may wish today to be   alluring and sensual as a dove. You may wish to be a powerful, conquering tiger and devour your enemy. You may be a gazelle, light and hesitant, a jolly lumbering bear, or a happy-go-lucky elephant. Or is it a snake you wish to be today? How good for your spine as, torturously and silently, you explore the forest. Or will you be a humming bird, hovering, darting, miraculously balancing while sipping nectar from a flower?

Is your element the sea? You may be the large, lazy whale, cruising slowly and majestically—or the legendary esthetic dolphin, leaping and playing. You may be in the mood to be a shark today. So *be* a shark. Consciously be a shark, here in your private sea, rather than unconsciously in the world of humans.

All the living creatures of sea, land and air are at your disposal, and all the past, present and future as well. You may be a prehistoric animal, or one of our own time, or one you imagine in a future evolution, perhaps even some strange creature living on a distant planet. There are no limits. You are the chooser.

Choose any one of the thousands upon thousands of living creatures—the one that expresses your mood today.

> Become this animal.
> Make the noises your animal makes.
> Feel as it feels.
> Think as it thinks.
> Eat as it eats.

Tunnel in the earth. Dive beneath the sea. Soar through the air. Climb and swing—creep and hide—leap and fly. You are one of natures's creations. Be the one you enjoy being, the one you wish to be.

> Then become one of the hated and despised animals.
> Be one of the frightening ones.
> Battle with your enemy. Destroy him. Eat him.

Children play this with the greatest gusto and naturalness. Play this game with them sometimes, but only if you can play it with a complete freedom. Do not impose your limitations on them. When you play with your children, do not be surprised if they become powerful and angry animals; let them win the fight; let them eat you up. They will feel so much better afterward, more peaceful and affectionate—and so will you.

One can do this recipe with music; find appropriate music for the animal and the mood.

It works—if you work

The recipes open the way to self-knowledge, then from self-knowledge to self-direction. Do not just read. Do and be.

23. ICE CUBES IN A FLOWING RIVER

You can make ice out of a flowing river. It is difficult, but it is possible. When the temperature goes low enough even Niagara Falls freezes solid. The same is true of life. If you bring down its temperature low enough it will begin to freeze. There are little frozen areas, ice cubes, in almost everyone's life.

Like a flowing river, each of us is continuously changing in a continuously changing world. Anything that is fixed, unchanging, frozen, is without life. The essence of life is its fluidity, its ability to change, to turn and take a new course. A frozen river cannot flow. In the same way, the frozen areas within ourselves block and impede the flow of our lives. In each ice cube a portion of our energy, a piece of our potential for living, is frozen.

What is an ice cube in our flowing river?

It may be a moment at the age of seven when, in front of a full class of children looking at me, I could not, simply could not, answer the teacher's question. At that particular moment, in that particular place, my world was those children enjoying my embarrassment; my world was that teacher, as powerful as God, asking that question, as important as life. And I failed—and froze. If I was a certain kind of sensitive child, and if this happened at a crucial time in my life or perhaps more than once, something in me froze then, and is still there, a fragment of my life, a little cube of ice. Today, many years later, it is still interfering with the easy flow of communication, still freezing me in the tongue-tied, paralyzing embarrassment of a child of seven. It is cold and hard; bring it out into the light and warmth of understanding, and it will melt.

What is an ice cube in our flowing river?

It may be a moment when a dear one died. Death is so final. How can I accept it? How can my own life continue to flow when such an important part of it is gone? So, unconsciously, in the wish to die with the beloved, a part of me freezes instead, freezes so hard that even tears may stop flowing. Tears that do not flow are tears that freeze within us, invisible, heavy, cold. Sometimes we are aware of something frozen and lifeless within us, sometimes we are not. Sometimes it is not only love for the lost one that makes us freeze; we may feel remorse because our love has not been unmixed, for it often happens that even the most devoted love is mingled with elements of irritation, resentment—in other words, of not-love. Death may freeze these conflicting emotions within us.

What is an ice cube in our flowing river?

It may be a distant moment when a baby stretched his arms toward Mommy, and Mommy did not notice. Or he was passionately longing for a caress from the strong hand of Daddy, who used that hand instead to light a cigarette. In that particular moment the touch of that strong hand would have fulfilled an urgent need for reassurance. But the hand was not given. Automatically and unconsciously the child's organism notices this—billions of cells notice the refusal of love. Usually this is only a passing incident; sometimes, because of the particular situation or because the experience is frequent, something inside freezes and later the adult finds it difficult to let his own affections flow. A discomfort, a vague impediment makes him stiffen, makes him uneasy or careful each time a feeling of warmth rises in him and seeks expression. Then when he attempts to express his feeling he does it so clumsily that often— alas, again—he is either unnoticed or misunderstood or rejected.

What is an ice cube in our flowing river?

It may be just one word—one word that froze in us a long, long time ago. For example, "doctor." What a magic word! And what power in that word! A long, long time ago a little boy fell from a tree; he was scared and hurt, and there was blood. Even stronger than his own pain and fear was the fear he felt in his mother or father. Seeing fear in an adult in whom he had his confidence was more frightening than the sight of his bloody knee. And now the all-powerful adult calls on another power: the doctor. "The doctor—if only we could find a doctor. Find a doctor— the doctor will know what to do. You be nice to the doctor; the doctor will fix it." In the child's mind the doctor is the Savior. This unconsciously remains in the adult, and almost anyone with the title of "doctor" makes him react, partially at least, with the preestablished notion that the doctor knows; the doctor will fix it. If the doctor did not come, or if he failed, there is another kind of reaction—just as conditioned and unrealistic. That is the reaction of the person who, without any fair examination, immediately decides that anyone who is a doctor either does not care—or is going to do no good—and charges for it besides. Doctor is just one of the *many* words around which ice cubes tend to form. Any words connected with professional standing or social authority can be a center of emotional crystallization. Here are a few of them: priest, minister, banker, count, policeman, general, director, chairman of the board etc. Many of us may be intimidated not only by some words representing professional and social status, but also by imposing uniforms signifying vested power.

To sum up, ice cubes stop the flow of life and energy; they confuse our thinking, limit our perceptions, and diminish our capacity to understand, to enjoy, to love. They are an emotional reaction of the past, frozen in place and never dislodged. At the time, the reaction had a certain logic. But the same reaction in the present is entirely irrational.

The purpose of this recipe is to dissolve these frozen emotions of the past, and liberate their imprisoned energy for living here and now.

Frozen emotions of the past show themselves in different ways; we can list them in categories like these:

Word blocks   Physical blocks
Perception blocks   Communication blocks
Intellectual blocks   Feeling blocks

As you follow the directions of the recipe and seek to uncover your own particular ice cubes, these labels may be useful to you; you may also think of other categories under which blocks may appear. Write them down. They are probably of particular significance to you.

Before you begin the recipe, make an agreement with yourself on two points:

First, that you, like almost everyone else, may be suffering or restricted in your life today because some part of you is frozen in a reaction of the past.

And second, that you will be honest in looking for and willing to dissolve any ice cube that you may find.

This may strike you as a curious precaution. But it is a fact that we become deeply attached to our emotional habit patterns and part with them only with the greatest reluctance, even when we know them to be irrational and costly to us in many ways.

Here are the directions:

Be sure that you will have at least one hour alone and undisturbed in a quiet place.

There are two ways to begin this recipe. Choose the way which you feel is more natural for you.

Either:

Imagine a flowing river.
Imagine it as vividly as you can.

Watch for a while as it flows so smoothly, serenely along.

Now you see some ice cubes floating by. Pick up the nearest one. Is it uncomfortably cold? Hold it for a moment, up to the light, and drop it.

What did you see in that cube of ice? A person? A word? An event? Yourself?

Or:

Think of an unwanted mood which you regularly feel in the presence of a certain person. Think of a recurrent reaction which takes place in a certain situation or when you hear certain words. Such recurrent moods or reactions are emotional ice cubes.

In either case:

> When did you experience that ice cube for the first time? Recently? A long time ago? It does not matter when it was. Re-live this moment of frozen emotion.
>
> Choose one moment, one event, one ice cube only. Re-live it completely. Repeat the words connected with it.
>
> Think and speak
>
> Think and see
>
> Think and smell
>
> Think and taste
>
> Live what you are doing
>
> Live what you are doing as completely as you can.

As you direct your attention to this person, situation, word, phrase, event, become aware of what is happening to your body.

> Do you feel tension in any muscles?
>
> Do you feel any change of temperature?
>
> Do you feel your body participating at all in your mental activity?

Now let your emotion take over. You have been thinking; you have been observing changes in your body. Now your emotion will complete the reality of the experience. Probably the emotion is a painful one; let it find its own form of expression. You may want to cry: then cry. You may want to laugh: then laugh. You may want to swear: then swear. It is by expressing your emotion that you will melt that ice. If the emotion can be expressed through other recipes, such as "The Tether Ball," "Bubble Freedom," etc., then use those recipes.

Repeat this sequence until you can relive the experience without any physical or emotional tensions.

Do the recipe, "Lay the Ghost."

In dissolving frozen emotions of the past you liberate and can use the energy imprisoned there. It is also very important to be alert in the present and not create new ice cubes.

When you feel tension around you or in you, when you are in a difficult situation, when events, feelings, or words are, or seem to be, against you—when you feel any part of you becoming unfree or frozen by something that is happening at that moment, ask yourself: *Am I making an ice cube now?*

It works—if you work

One can read the recipes—
    understand the recipes—
    know the recipes—
    like the recipes—
    analyze the recipes—
    experience the recipes.
Experiencing the recipes is the true, creative way to evaluate them.

24. EMERGENCY!

Often, almost miraculously, our creative potential comes forth with irresistible power and intelligence when we are in a state of emergency.

To save someone she loves, a frail woman may show the courage of a tigress and the strength of a trained athlete. To avert an automobile accident, a driver may accomplish in a split second a feat of thinking, visual judgment and skill that would have taken him weeks to plot and practice.

In a community emergency, a flood, a fire, a war, many ordinary men and women find themselves performing acts of genuine heroism.

An emergency brings about a profound change in our characters; what is trivial, insignificant, irrelevant, drops away in an instant.

Possibly you have experienced a moment of emergency in which you saw someone, perhaps yourself, accomplish a feat of muscle or mind that saved a situation, or a life.

So many good things emerge in us, in an emergency. How can we produce artificially in ourselves this psychophysical state which permits us to use our latent creative potentials without one of the major ingredients of emergency, that is, without danger? To do this completely is impossible. But it is not impossible to produce a state of emergency in a measure that is efficacious without being dangerous. Our primary need is for AIR. Anything that prevents us from breathing threatens our life, and is therefore experienced as a major emergency.

Try this for yourself. Take a deep, an enormous breath. Fill your lungs completely. Hold the breath as long as possible, and then a little longer. Now expel the air, slowly. Empty your lungs, more, more: let out the last little puff of air until you are all empty. And now that you are all, completely empty—stay empty. Do not take a breath—not yet—not yet—do not permit yourself to breathe, stay empty to the very limit of your endurance ———— NOW! let the air rush in.

In those few seconds when you deliberately stop breathing, you are more or less in a state of emergency. In those few eternal seconds all your thirty trillions of cells seem to be shouting, "Air, air, air!" (Actually, your cells are not yet deprived; that imperious demand is a reflex mechanism that reacts automatically to the carbon dioxide level in your blood. But the effect is as clamorous as thirty trillion cells with one voice.)

For those few seconds when you were deprived of air nothing else mattered except breathing.

Think, now, of your present concern, or question, or problem; put it into a single word or name. For example:

Job
Health
Wife
Husband
Time

> Loneliness
> Money
> Pain

Now your question or concern or problem is condensed into one word or name. That word or name stands for all your thoughts or feelings about the state of affairs that is disturbing you.

Here is the sequence; practice it lying down:

> In a single word or name, express your question, concern, or problem.
>
> Mentally repeating that word, filll your lungs to their extreme capacity.
>
> Mentally repeating that word, keep the air in your lungs as long as you comfortably can.
>
> Mentally repeating that word, slowly let the air come out through your mouth, all the air out, all of it—
>
> Mentally repeating that word, make sure there is no more air in you; expel the last of it by sounding the letter ESS for as long as you can.
>
> Mentally repeating that word, pull in your abdomen and hold the muscles tight.
>
> Be watchful. The natural tendency is to take a breath through your nose without being aware of it.
>
> Mentally repeating that word, remain empty and without motion as long as you can—as your cells cry for air, keep repeating that word—when you cannot possibly hold out any longer—breathe! Let the longed-for air flow into you like a river of luminous energy, revitalizing every cell in your body.

What is the point of all this? What are the results to expect? Here are a few of the things that may happen.

In this context of life-and-death emergency, your problem in all probability will change proportion. By focussing on your problem in such a way you set your subconscious to work on it, and thus you may get a completely new view of it from your deep mind.

The physiological effect of this kind of breathing, combined with the psychological approach, is very powerful. You will feel an increased mental activity and vigor, a physical exhilaration, a renewal of life flowing into you. You will become aware that the ordinary automatic process of breathing can be transformed into a most wonderful, conscious act.

Even for those who have no problem this is an excellent recipe. Try it.

Note: This is a powerful recipe; do not overdo it. If you have, or suspect you have, any weakness of heart or lungs, consult your physician.

It works—if you work

After a period of honest work with the recipes, you will automatically forget yourself, for when you solve the problem of yourself you forget yourself and go on to other things, other people.

25. ARE YOU CULTIVATING TODAY YOUR NEUROSIS OF TOMORROW?

Do you *always* lose things?
Does she *always* forget appointments?
Do your children *always* make the same mistakes?
Is he (she) *always* irritable on Sundays?
Are people *always* taking advantage of you?

Any one of these may happen frequently. When we say over and over that it *always* happens, we assume, consciously or not, that it will inevitably happen.

In all probability it will.

Here are the links in this crippling chain.

In the past this event has frequently occurred.

We make a habit of asserting that this event always occurs.

This repeated assertion acts as an unconscious suggestion to ourselves.

This suggestion results in our conscious or unconscious acceptance of the fact that the event will inevitably recur.

By accepting the event as inevitable we feel exonerated of all responsibility.

We also, consciously or not, collaborate; we actually pave the way for the event to occur again and again.

In little and big ways, chains of compulsion like this are encouraged. The neurosis of tomorrow is fed on the collective as well as the individual level. Whole nations can be led into self-destructive behavior by demagogic leaders, slanted news, false and incomplete information. Here, however, we will deal with personal ways of cultivating neurosis. There are three:

I may be cultivating today *my* neurosis of tomorrow.

I may be cultivating today *other people's* neurosis of tomorrow.

I may be allowing other people to cultivate *my* neurosis of tomorrow.

How do I cultivate my neurosis of tomorrow? For example:

I often forget appointments.

I repeat to myself that I *always* forget appointments.

I do not keep an engagement book in which I write my appointment down.

If I keep a diary I do not look at it.

The outcome is that I forget appointments—and excuse myself by saying with a sweet smile, "You see? That's how I am! I always forget appointments!" And so I give another turn to the vicious circle; I reinforce the chain of compulsion. I also irritate all those with whom I have dealings, and perpetuate in their minds a childish, irresponsible image of myself.

Another example: I am unkind to someone today. I do not apologize or atone in any way. I make no effort to undo what I have done. All I do is continue to think and worry about my unkindness and its possible consequences. I nourish a feeling of guilt from which I will suffer tomorrow and tomorrow and tomorrow. Another revolution of the vicious circle.

Or: I cannot find things. I keep them in such an unsystematic way that quite logically they cannot be found. I go on losing things, and I go on distributing them about so unsystematically that only a clairvoyant could find them. Another turn of the vicious circle.

I have difficulty finding what I want in stores. I set out saying that I will not get any shopping done, convincing myself that I will not get any shopping done. Then I go to a store which is very unlikely to have the merchandise I am looking for. I return home saying that I never get any shopping done. Another whirl of the vicious circle.

In my work I must often have luncheon conferences with my superior. I am a conscientious worker, but I am dependent on his approval for my job security, and these luncheons are tense occasions for me. I announce in advance that I am lunching with my boss and as usual I end up having indigestion. Knowing that I am tense, do I order carefully, choosing simple dishes that are easy to digest? Do I eat little, and slowly? No. I order heavy "masculine" (that is, fried) food, bolt it unthinkingly in big mouthfuls, and suffer the consequences in a miserable afternoon, no dinner, and a depressed evening. The circumstances of my tense luncheon are beyond my control. But the way in which I deal with them guarantees me a perfect opportunity to give another twirl to the vicious circle, forge another link in the compulsive chain.

How do I cultivate other people's neurosis? As a parent I may do this quite unknowingly. Let us say that my child has a poor appetite. I am genuinely concerned about this; I comment on it, I complain, I worry aloud. The atmosphere at meals is not conducive to good appetite, so that the child eats even more poorly than usual. I threaten punishment and promise rewards. The child becomes aware that he has some power over me, that what he does at mealtime makes him important. He does not think this out or plan it. He would change if he could, but if I approach mealtime tomorrow with the same apprehension I have today, the child will probably react in the same way, and give me solid reason for my apprehension. And again I will react in ways that will upset the child's appetite and attitude toward food, his associations with it, his digestion. Thus instead of being a means of leasure and nourishment, eating becomes so involved with a sequence of negative emotions that food itself is transformed into a negative emotion.

In adults one can often retrace and correct the cause of digestive disturbances in a vicious circle that began very early in childhood.

Here are some other examples:

To someone who should not be drinking liquor I offer tempting drinks. Probably I congratulate myself for being a gracious hostess. But I am really guilty of a stupid unkindness to my guest.

The same situation occurs with those who are trying to lose weight. So often have I seen the most tempting, fattening desserts offered to the would-be reducer. Surely this is feeding today someone else's neurosis of tomorrow.

It is easy to keep an employee insecure and fearful, simply by talking often, not to him but within his hearing, of the necessity for reducing expenses and personnel.

To his wife, insecure about her clothes, a husband may often make remarks about the easy, inexpensive elegance of another woman.

To her husband, unsatisfied and insecure about his income, a wife may observe how much money almost anybody can make nowadays.

Withholding news from someone anxiously waiting for it is a particular form of cultivating another's neurosis. Nurtured by silence, anxiety and fear are bound to grow. Even when good news finally arrives, the psychological disturbance of prolonged anxiety is not completely dispelled.

Of a child insecure and poor in arithmetic, ask the multiplication table *in the presence of others.* Probably the child will answer incorrectly, or will not be able to answer at all. This humiliating failure can make a deep mark on a child; he may for the rest of his life have difficulties related to that early, apparently insignificant experience.

There are a thousand ways to keep a person's neurosis alive today and nourish it for a more devilish life tomorrow. Some people do this deliberately with fiendish awareness of others' weaknesses. It is so easy to nourish the canker of fear, the ulcer of inferiority—it is so easy to overpower the opponent by striking at the weakest point, physical or mental. And often this is prefaced by the words: "Dear, I do this for your *own* good." More often the evil is done unconsciously, but the results are equally painful and destructive.

How do I allow others to cultivate my neurosis? We need only go back to the examples just given and reverse the role. I may be tempted by my hostess with drinks and foods. I may be the insecure employee, the wife worried about her clothes, the husband worried about his income.

For these situations, the recipe that is perfectly suited is "You Are Not the Target." With that recipe, in combination with the present one, we discover that we need not allow others to feed our neurosis. We need not respond in the automatic, damaging way to another's damaging behavior. We can break our own and the other's neurotic chain reaction. When we convert harmful energy to good use, we can be both keener and kinder.

The general direction for this recipe is to pay attention to what we do to ourselves and others—to become aware. It is against our ethical principles as human beings to harm others. But aside from ethics, it is against our self-interest. The neurosis we cultivate in others inevitably rebounds against ourselves. From heavy-handed authority resentment and rebellion will develop. From sexual repression or dissatisfaction, anger, nervous tension and its consequences will arise. From religious or ideological fanaticism, ignorance and bigotry will develop and infect everything around themselves. If we nourish someone else's neurosis or fear, it is almost inevitable that we will, sooner or later, be hurt by it ourselves.

Here are the directions for this recipe:

> Recall the unwanted events or reactions in your life that are always happening.
>
> Make a list of them.

Choose one that you want to be rid of. For clarity let us call it "Event A."

There is at least one recurring factor to Event A every time it happens. It may be a word, a thought, a physical sensation, a person, a place, anything.

Above all, there is a feeling that is always present before Event A happens. This feeling may be obvious or subtle, easily definable or difficult to pin down.

It is of this feeling that we must become aware.

The following questions will help you to accomplish that.

What do I always feel, think, act, or say before Event A happens?

Who is present?

What is said or done?

What happens to my relationship to that person or persons?

Do I receive any benefit, any obvious or hidden satisfaction?

How does my body feel and function before Event A happens?

What is the common factor always present in Event A and the feeling that goes along with it?

Find that feeling; locate it in your body-mind.

Now use and transform this feeling. Any of the following recipes will help you do that: "The Art of Converting Energy," "Bubble Freedom," "Tether Ball," "TLA-TLA-TLA." These are the most direct, but you may find among the other recipes one that suits the feeling specifically.

The best time to practice this recipe is immediately after Event A happens.

If you become suddenly aware that Event A is just about to happen, or is happening again, *stop everything*.

Stop thoughts, words, actions.

Instead, focus keenly all your attention on the antics of your fascinating automatic self! See how it wants you to say those words; your mouth almost says them—but you don't permit it. See how your body wants to make certain movements; it almost does—but you stop it. That automatic self has been in command for so long. It has said those words, performed those actions hundreds, maybe thousands of times. But you need not follow that orchestra composed of your emotions, your thoughts, your conditioned reflex. Of course the orchestra wants to play the same old piece, the same old worn-out nonsense that it plays without a conductor. But today, suddenly and powerfully the conductor is present:—*it is you*. And you direct your orchestra to play another piece, a new one, a fresh one. Surprise the orchestra. Surprise everybody! *You* are the conductor; you change the old tune. *You* transform the vicious circle into an ascending spiral.

It works—if you work

At the beginning you will need the full time that is suggested to do each recipe. Do not begrudge those few hours. Think of the years you spend to build up your career, your home, your environment, everything outside of you. Only a fraction of that time is asked now to build up yourself. It is only if you are well integrated that you can enjoy the environment you have built for yourself.

After you have experienced and absorbed the recipes they will require less time as you will know how to use them every day in living.

26. *YOUR IMAGINATION IS YOURS*

"Oh, say, can you see?" asks the author of "The Star-Spangled Banner."

Let us elaborate a little on his question.

When you sing the national anthem, what *can* you see with your mind's eye?

Are you able to visualize the dawn's early light, the greenish sky, the golden glow behing the hill, the black silhouettes of trees or houses, the rosy clouds? Can you actually perceive the redness of the rocket's red glare? Or the redness of the stripes on the wind-whipped flag? Or the white stars and their dark blue ground?

Some people can see these things with their inner eye just as clearly as they can see them with their physical eyes. Others see them only dimly, only with difficulty. A few insist that they cannot see them at all.

Some people find it hard to see with the mind's eye, but have no difficulty hearing with the mind's ear, smelling with the mind's nose, touching with the mind's fingertips and tasting with the mind's tongue and palate. Perhaps you are one of those. You may not be able to see the rocket's red glare, but you can hear the rocket's whoosh and bang; you can smell the gunpowder smoke; you can feel the coolness of the dawn wind on your face.

And, as we all know, these perceptions are always more than mere perceptions. They are accompanied by feelings and memories. They evoke associations. They start trains of thought. They trigger sudden insights.

Psychologists make a distinction between "reproductive imagination"—the revival of past perceptions of particular objects—and "productive imagination" which is the power of combining images of past perceptions in new, useful and creative ways.

We see, then, that the word "imagination" covers an enormously wide spectrum of mental activity. At the lower end of this spectrum is the simple ability to see some familiar object with the mind's eye; at the upper end, we find the greatest works of productive imagination in the fields of art and science.

However creativity is not the monopoly of the Shakespeares and Einsteins of this world. There is a science of intelligent living, an art of being fully human, in which we all can and ought to be creative.

To use our imagination is part of the total *art of being*. To imagine other people's imagination is part of the *art of being with others*.

To realize how other people imagine, I propose a game. Try it alone, or with one friend or many, at a party with children or grownups. It will show you the wide variations of the human imagination. It will amuse you and your friends.

Ask them to close their eyes and sing, silently to themselves, "The Star-Spangled Banner," and when they have finished, to open their eyes.

Then ask: What happened to you? What did you see, think, imagine, and feel as you were listening with your mind's ear to your own silent singing?

The responses will be surprisingly varied.

For one person it will be absolutely natural to see the entire scene, while the next will think you are joking.

One will be moved only by imagining the music, paying no attention to the words, while for another the words alone will evoke images and historical situations.

Sometimes the national anthem may be felt exclusively as a physical experience; one might feel the rigidity of his body, his feet firm on the hard earth, the rain slanting down against his face while, as a soldier, he stands at attention to the music.

Some will feel the wind that is waving the banner; others will only see the symbols of war and victory.

Some will be absorbed in a personal situation and personal emotions that the anthem evokes. For others the response may be not personal but rather that strong, stirring general emotion that bands and patriotic songs arouse.

All the while, on the outside, nothing is happening; in silence, each person is simply imagining the sounds and words of the anthem and whatever they evoke in his interior universe.

It is difficult to be able to imagine how other people imagine. It requires not only imagination but also insight into other people's reactions. It is difficult for a person whose imagination is connected with body feelings to grasp that, for another, physical sensations exist only in the reality of the present time. On the other hand, for that very person, the memory of a color seen twenty years ago may be today as vivid as the original perception.

Imagination can be directed, and this is one of the purposes of this recipe.

Your Imagination is Yours

It belongs to you, not you to it.

Imagination is a mysterious gift of which we should be the masters, not the slaves.

Imagine what life would be like without imagination! There would be no Michelangelo or Da Vinci, no Edison, no delinquents and no saints, no Mozart, no nuclear power.

Geniuses and saints are the product of an alliance of imagination with good will, talent, discipline and other fruitful qualities. On the destructive side the alliance of imagination with ignorance and ill will, with fear or envy brings forth a monstrous brood of every kind of evil.

In an article on the psychology of the imagination, Frank Baron writes: "Indeed, when we imagine divinity, we impute to it the power to have imagined *us*, and by an act of will to have created us. Ever since man became conscious of himself, imagination has had in it something of mystery and magic, and has seemed a process which cannot be completely understood." *

In this recipe we will not deal with the extremes of imagination as—together with many other factors—it manifests itself in saints or criminals, geniuses or fanatics. Here we are concerned with the use of imagination in our daily life.

Like any other faculty, imagination can be starved and suffocated or stimulated and nourished.

Some people say, "I just don't have imagination."

* "The Psychology of Imagination," Frank Baron. *Scientific American,* September 1958.

Wait. Do not give up too hastily. Sometimes the imagination is there, but it has been put away in a dusty attic. At one time there may have been good reason; the very people who think of themselves as unimaginative may be the ones who have the richest imagination. As children they may have had such free, unhampered imagination that they neglected or distorted reality, to the bafflement of adults.

That caused trouble, perhaps a spanking and the accusation: "You're a little liar."

Then, possibly without being aware of what he was doing, the victim of too much imagination decided that the cost of imaginative living was just too high. So the world of imagination was locked up in the attic and at its door a label was nailed. The words on the label may differ but their meaning is more or less the same: "Dangerous—don't touch." "You're bad." "You're a liar." "You never tell the truth." "He's crazy, always imagining things." Besides the memory of such words there may also be the remembered shame and physical pain of spanking. Usually people who have had this experience unconsciously pass it on to their children.

There are of course very good reasons to be wary of imagination. It is a gift full of destructive as well as creative potentialities. Here are a few everyday examples of imagination destructively used:

> A wife believes and complains that her husband is stingy —yet the fact is that he has always given her all the money he makes.

> A husband lives in the constant fear that his wife is going to leave him—yet the fact is that she has been with him for twenty years.

> An overprotective mother imagines that her grownup
> son is incapable of solving his problems—yet the fact
> is that his life is running smoothly and he is well and
> happy.

Other factors besides imagination are of course involved
in these erroneous judgments. But in all of them, misdirected imagination plays an important part.

Imagination is powerful. If it is persistently misdirected
it will make its evil fancies come true.

A man, finally tired of accusations of stinginess, may stop
giving all his money to his wife. And a wife, feeling the
constant tension of a possessive husband, will finally rebel
and leave him. Then the victims of these situations will
say, "I was right!" Probably it would be more correct to say,
"I made it come true, and it serves me right."

In any kind of propaganda, good or bad, the tools of the
propagandist are designed to awaken, excite, and direct the
imagination of the public. The great industries spend millions for advertising purposes to stimulate the potential
buyer's imagination, and through the imagination to create
desire for ownership.

When one begins to think about the good uses of imagination, one is confronted with the fact that almost everything that is good is partly the work of imagination. From
a great bridge to a chemical discovery, from beautiful music to a lively story, from a good soup to a social reform—
in all human achievements imagination has a place of
honor.

Let us use this wonderful faculty to our own advantage.
For example, if you are not satisfied with your figure or
posture, do this several times a day for a period of days or
weeks. It takes only a few seconds:

Close your eyes. Imagine a mirror.

Project, in that mirror, the image of yourself with the figure you can and wish to have; project yourself with the posture you can and wish to have.

If you do this, you can expect that your figure and posture will become more and more like the one you project. (Do not project the impossible. See the recipe, "TLA-TLA-TLA.")

We should train ourselves in the use of imagination when we are well, so that we are ready to use it when we are not.

In medical practice, in all times and all countries, imagination has been used, sometimes badly, sometimes well. An illustration of a good use of the imagination is the placebo. In medical language, a pill with no active ingredient is called a placebo. The patient is told that the pill will make him well, although in fact it contains nothing that will change his physical condition. When it is wisely used the placebo can be most valuable, not only for diagnosis but also because the patient may get well without taking powerful drugs.

Between 25 and 35 percent of patients in physical pain are completely relieved by a placebo, which actually contains no ingredient to alleviate pain. An additional 30 percent of the patients enjoy some relief. About one-third are not affected.

What is the difference among these three groups of people?

The most complete array of scientific researchers could not answer this question completely today. However, we can say that the group which receives benefit from the placebo is endowed with these qualities:

A vivid imagination.

An imagination that can be directed (the direction being the doctor's words: "This pill will make you feel better") and—

An organic connection between the imaginative processes and the physiological processes. Exactly how this connection works is still a mystery.

The fortunate people who receive benefit from a placebo show us in the clearest possible way that body and mind are one.

For those who enjoy and can direct their powers of imagination, this recipe is fun and easy to follow.

But do not imagine that it is only for the imaginative! On the contrary, those who imagine that they are *not* imaginative are precisely the ones who will derive the greatest benefits from this recipe.

But first, a caution: the more we use our imaginative powers and give them free rein, the more clearly we must become aware of reality; the more alert and quick we must be in knowing the difference between fact and fancy.

It is an error to think that imagination is incompatible with facts. The most fruitful imagination is that which makes use of facts, and recombines them in creative ways. People had seen apples falling and had been watching the movement of the moon thousands of years. Then Newton observed these two apparently unrelated facts and used his imagination to create the all-embracing theory of universal gravitation. Analogously out of the chaos of fragments of memory and given facts, saints and poets create aesthetic, intellectual or moral order.

Let us imagine facts as a Greek colonnade made of imperishable marble. From one column to the other, moving in the wind, there are climbing roses, their roots in the earth, their fragrance lifting to the sky, their branches embracing the solid columns. Marble and roses, facts and imagination. From their embrace springs creative living.

And now the first directions for this recipe:

> If you believe that you do not have imagination, think of a person whom you consider endowed with this quality.
>
> Jump into his place.

If, in any way, you feel uneasy about imagination, turn to the recipe "Throw Words Away." Practice those directions, using the following phrases:

> "That is all your imagination."
>
> "You are a liar."
>
> "Stop telling fibs."
>
> "Stop imagining things."

Or use any word or phrase that you feel is connected with the faculty of inventing or imagining. The connection may be vague or even hidden, but if you feel as if there is any connection at all, go ahead.

If you feel you have imagination but you cannot direct it, practice the recipe "TLA-TLA-TLA."

Many other recipes in the book will help you to free, direct and enjoy your imagination.

Do not be troubled if you cannot immediately use and direct your imagination. It has been kept in a cast for so many years! What would you have to do if you wanted to use again a limb that had been immobilized in a cast for a long time?

First, you would have to decide that you wanted the cast removed.

Second, you would have to find the tools to remove the cast.

Third, you would have to care for the poor ex-prisoner, give it sun and exercise.

Anyone who has had to wear a cast even for six or eight weeks knows how long it takes to bring that part of the body back to health and strength.

The same is true of imagination. First, decide to free it from its cast. Second, use the tools necessary to remove the cast. ("Throw Words Away" is one. This and other recipes mentioned will make you freer of the cast and more capable of using your imaginative potentials.) Third, give sun and air and exercise to your imagination. Direct it, enjoy it —play with it.

If you feel that your imagination is free, that it belongs to you and not you to it—then play with it. Here are some ways. Try them and then imagine others.

> Do some of the things that the creators of fairy tales and myths used to do. Imagine centaurs, mermaids, dragons, elephant-headed gods. Imagine witches riding on broomsticks, turbaned Orientals sailing through the air on magic carpets.

> Look at a wall on which a painting is hanging. Close your eyes and imagine that wall without the painting.

> Look at the room you are in, and with your imagination rearrange all the furniture. Imagine the room painted in different colors. Imagine how this room would be in a different house, in a different country.

Now go back and relive a bad, frightening experience of childhood or adult life. For instance, imagine an unpleasant discussion you had with someone who was trying to dominate you.

Do it this way:

> *See him or her with a ridiculous hat.*
>
> *See him or her, not as one individual, but multiplied by six: six ridiculously comic figures instead of one single, frightening one.*
>
> *Imagine the serious, dignified, imperturbable person, who feels so superior to you, compelled—absolutely and utterly compelled—to put his finger in his nose while he is speaking so authoritatively to you about how you should behave.*

Infinity and eternity are the limits of imagination. You can project your imagination into the past or into the future; you can destroy an old image that has troubled you or create a new one that will rejoice you.

Here are some of the ways in which to play. Do them. Enjoy them. Find other ways of your own. Some of these may strike you as childish, and they are. They come straight out of childhood, when imagination is free and unfettered. They may help you to recapture that freedom.

Imagine that:

> *All your joints are moving on perfect ball bearings, annointed with fragrant precious golden oil. Everything is smooth, round, gold.*

Or that:

> *You and everybody has a sunflower, right in the center of his being. Let us have this sunflower exactly where*

the solar plexus—or sun plexus—is. Now, feel your golden, resplendent, powerful sunflower right in the center of you.

Now see the golden, resplendent, powerful sunflower right in the center of everybody else. Infinite golden sunflower—it has a center and transcends its own center.

Now go out into the world, into the crowded, embittered, tired world of greedy and frightened humanity, and yet, with your imagination, you see and feel the sunflower in the center of yourself and everyone.

You speak to people while you feel your sunflower, their sunflower. And now, the sunflowers begin to communicate with each other. No matter what your conversation above the solar plexus is, pleasant or not, irritated or insincere, the sunflowers carry on their conversation, their communication from solar plexus to solar plexus.

Perhaps the person who is speaking to you only wants to get something out of you—the sunflowers continue their conversation. Perhaps you are bored to tears by your conversation—no matter, sunflowers do not know boredom. Perhaps you are speaking to someone to whom you have given much, and just now, in this conversation, this person only wants to harm you—sunflowers have no idea of such a miserable, complicated relationship.

No matter how silly or malicious our oral conversation, the sunflowers silently communicate. In spite of our chatter, they communicate like drops of water flowing in the same river, a golden river of communication from sunflower to sunflower.

This was used by a well-known diplomat who was able to navigate through international intrigue and preserve his health and love of life. Do not discuss this recipe with other people. Just do it.

Or imagine that:

>When you are walking, you are hanging from a star.
>
>Your star is a magnet and exercises a lifting power over your body.
>
>Your head responds to the irresistable attraction of your stellar magnet.
>
>It is taking all the weight off your feet—and you just glide along, light and free, carried by your star.
>
>Only you and your star know this.

Don't tell anyone your starry secret.

It works—if you work

Certain recipes are not easy. You may refuse what is asked of you. This refusal has an ambivalent quality: it protects you from undertaking more than you can handle, but it also limits the benefit you can receive from the recipes.

Be aware of your refusal; neither give in to it nor fight it. Continue doing the recipe with essential honesty and awareness.

27. HELP ME, FOR I ENVY YOU

There are many kinds of envy.

The destitute people of the slums of Calcutta or Palermo envy the comfortable people of Manhattan and Hollywood. There is nothing to do about that envy but take away its cause.

There is another kind of envy. It is the envy we feel for those who are more endowed by nature than we are. Obviously nature does not distribute equally her gifts. Many people are better looking than we are, have more brilliant minds, more productive talent. Yet each one of us has a function to fulfill. It is when we spend our time and energy looking down in contempt or looking up with sterile longing that we lose sight of this function. Envy is comparison. He who is in the continuous process of being and becoming what he really is, directs his attention to real values, not to measuring other people's achievements.

But if a child who has been hungry all his life sees a fat child gorge himself with candy it is only natural that the hungry one would passionately and violently try to take away that candy. It is no use to explain to the hungry child that it is not the other child's fault that he eats too much, to explain to him the social system of which both overweight and undernourished children are victims; and it is no use to give him recipes—the first thing to do is to give him *food*.

On the other hand if a woman who has one mink is envious of another who has two, the *one* thing *not* to do is to give her another mink coat. What the envious woman needs is a magic mirror in which she can see the destitute, starving creature inside of her who makes her feel she wants another fur coat. Magic mirrors are not for sale, but fortunately we all have one, a built-in one. But it is hard for us to look into the magic mirror; and when we finally summon enough courage to look, so much stands between our honest willing eyes and the clear reflection in the mirror—our conditioning and our fears, our physiological, chemical, emotional make-up, and social structure in which we live—almost everything stands between us and the clear reflection in the mirror. Almost everything—yet not enough to stop that part of us that nothing can stop.

It is difficult to look into the magic mirror and say, "I see envy." Envy disguises itself in more acceptable cloaks such as self-disparagement, righteous indignation, adulation.

Envy is composed of several emotional ingredients, the most important of which are:

Fear
Desire to win
Desire to own
Desire to dispossess others
Desire for improvement

From this partial list we can see that even envy, one of the most cruel expressions of the ego against itself, has a good element in it—desire for improvement. In itself, the desire to own is neither good nor bad, for it is only when this natural drive takes unnatural proportions that it becomes harmful.

The two malignant elements are: Fear—which is basic to almost all negative emotion, and desire to dispossess others —which is the specific and worse side of envy. It was the tragedy of Iago—his envy of Othello drove him to plot the destruction of a man whose only offence was to be happier and more gifted than himself. It was a piece of gratuitous wickedness which brought no advantage to the envious criminal.

One of the most enlightening approaches to the question of envy is discussed in Krishnamurti's article, *The Fragmentation of Man is Making Him Sick* (Commentaries on Living—3rd series). I strongly suggest that you read this piece for many reasons, one being that Krishnamurti's approach to envy is different from the one in this recipe.

My own approach is as follows:

> Define what the word envy is to you, what feelings it arouses, what remembrances, what faces, what voices the word "envy" evokes in you. There are three possibilities:
>
> You will immediately know that you are, or have been, envious of someone.
>
> You will be uncertain.
>
> You will decide that you never have been and/or are not envious of anyone. If you know for sure you are not envious, ignore this recipe.
>
> If you find yourself uncertain whether or not you are envious, then think and feel, during the time allowed for this recipe, as you imagine an envious person would think and feel. If this comes easily then go on the

assumption that you are capable of envy. If it feels completely unnatural then skip this recipe.

Admit to yourself that you are envious.
Acknowledge who it is that you envy.

Feel the envy and the person who evokes it. Re-live a time when you were particularly envious. See, hear, feel this person. You may have to get the feeling connected with him out of your system by punching a tether ball, by dancing, or by blowing it out as in "Bubble Freedom."

Now look at what is left of your envy, and list the ingredients of which it is made: fear, desire to disposses another, desire to own, desire for improvement, or any other ingredients not listed here.

This is one of the best opportunities to apply the principle of the transformation of energy; take the energy contained in the negative ingredients and use it to reinforce the positive ingredients. Transform the painful feeling of envy in a creative action which will absorb all your attention. Read again Chapter 2, "Transformation of Energy," and the recipe "The Art of Converting Energy."

By now you will probably have freed yourself of the pain of the envy, and begun some good, interesting project which is making you a happier, better, more interesting human being. How wonderful and how possible it is to use that extraordinary force contained in envy to do something beautiful and pleasant, like swimming or playing tennis, doing a sculpture, planting a tree or some flowers.

It is rare that envy still persists after such a treatment; if it does there is one more thing you can do. It takes courage to do it, but the rewards are immense. It is this: go to the person of whom you are envious and say, "Look, I am envious of you. The reason may be real or imaginary, but my suffering is real—it diminishes me and it can be of no good to you or anyone else. My pain will spread as an infectious disease unless something is done about it. Apparently you are, even if unwittingly, the cause of this hurt—therefore you are also the one who can help it. Please do." This is the idea. Express it in your own way. The worst that can happen is that you may not be understood, but your honesty and courage in communicating with the object of your envy have already made you freer and stronger. It is more likely that the other person will respond well to your appeal and a pleasant, fruitful relationship will develop. If you ever find yourself in the position of this other person, use the recipe "Jump Into the Other's Place." Then you will realize what it is to feel envy, and what it takes to come bravely out into the open and ask for help. For the envious person it is this courage that is of value. It is not the other person's reaction that is important, it is your action, your candid courage in saying:

Help Me, for I Envy You

Go on—do it.

You have nothing to lose but your pain.

It works—if you work

Pain, confusion, fear—these you can alleviate, clarify, dispel, by your work with the recipes.

If you are reading this you are looking for something. This may be it.

28.   *TENDER IS THE NIGHT*

Yes, tender is the night when, fulfilled and grateful, you lie near the loved one.

Tender is the night when, ecstatically, you listen to the breathing of the one you love becoming quieter and lighter.

Tender is the night when two are asleep as one.

Then, we need no recipe.

But when the night is lonely and frightening—when tenderness does not seem of this world—when sleeplessness is sapping the last remnant of that vanishing strength that we so badly need—when the night presents at once all our problems and no possible solution—when the night seems a dark gray voyage with no motion, purpose or end—

Then this recipe will help.

It would require an encyclopedia, not a single recipe, to describe and analyze all the causes of bad nights.

These causes range from poor digestion to unsolved situations, from bitter feelings to improper food, from uncomfortable sleeping conditions to overactive thoughts or an uncongenial sleeping companion.

The recipes deal with many of the basic causes of bad nights such as restlessness, fear, lack of love. If you have bad nights for reasons you are aware of, I feel certain that you can find among the recipes those which deal with the causes of your trouble.

This recipe is for those of us, and indeed there are many, who cannot put a finger on any specific cause, and yet they cannot sleep.

Falling asleep is a mysterious process. The body does not need sleep; it only needs rest. It is our daytime consciousness, the cortical brain, that needs to be stilled and silenced for seven or for the eight hours out of the twenty-four. Yet it is often the body, not the mind, that keeps us from sleeping.

When we are awake there is a continuous exchange of messages—nervous stimuli—between the body and the mind. The brain sends its orders. The muscles, tensing and relaxing as we move about, notify the brain of what they are doing. The senses also send their messages, millions of them. Most of these the brain ignores because they are familiar and require no attention.

In the gentle, natural subsidence into sleep, this exchange of messages between body and mind gradually slows down, like a conversation between two drowsy people. If our sleeping conditions are well arranged, our senses bring us only pleasant, reassuring messages; our muscles relax and send fewer and fewer messages of movement; the brain puts aside the day's activities and sends a diminishing number of messages to the muscles. And so, sleep comes.

If either the brain or the body refuses to slow down, then we are wakeful.

Falling asleep must have presented few problems to primitive man, who spent most of his days in strenuous physical activity. His tired muscles gratefully relaxed; without the body's alerting messages, his brain quieted its thinking, and he slept. For us, who spend our days mainly in sitting—at desks, in cars, in living rooms—the muscles are often tense but not tired, not ready or able to relax.

And then come the thoughts that keep us even more wakeful, that keep sending disturbing messages to our muscles, preventing them from relaxing. And so, the cycle of sleeplessness is set in motion, tense muscles evoking restless thoughts, restless thoughts evoking tenseness in the muscles.

What can we do?

We must break into the dialogue between mind and muscles. We may do this by way of the muscles or by way of the mind, or both.

First of all we should realize that it is not so much the quantity of sleep that matters—*it is the quality*. We have all had nights of heavy, torpid sleep, only to awaken feeling more tired and depressed than when we went to bed. And most of us have known the delicious feeling of freshness and vitality that follows the briefest of naps.

A good use of the last hour before we go to sleep will benefit us in two ways. Instead of resenting the period of wakefulness we shall find it interesting and rewarding; at the same time we shall discover that we have improved the quality of our sleep. For the quality of our sleep depends in large measure on the state of our body-mind during the hour or so before we go to sleep. As sleep approaches, the partition between conscious and unconscious becomes thinner and thinner, and disturbing thoughts can easily break through into the deeper regions of the mind. For this reason we must be particularly aware of how we deal with our thoughts and feelings at bedtime. This is even more important for children than for adults.

In this recipe are seven methods for inviting sleep and also improving its quality. Many of them can also be used during the day. A daytime nap gives us practically a double day of energy. One of the most rewarding skills we can learn is the napping skill.

Besides the sleep recipes here the "TLA-TLA-TLA" is often effective in overcoming sleeplessness. So is "Dance Naked With Music," which prepares you for sleep by redirecting the body's physical energies and by releasing emotional tensions.

Here are several well-tried approaches to better sleep. Each has its own title to facilitate a quick recollection and identification. Give these a test and invent others.

As You Like It

As soon as you are comfortably in bed, silence the chattering of your daytime mind and enter the world of creative imagination: embark upon an adventure of muscular and sensory enjoyment.

For example, go in imagination to the beach. (This is a favorite of mine.) Feel the edge of the beach where the waves gently wash up on the sand. Feel the soft, wet sand under your feet. The water is clear, transparent, inviting. In the beginning, you walk leisurely, slowly; then, becoming invigorated, you quicken your pace. You walk effortlessly—lightly—faster and faster. Now you break into a run—running, running on the wet sand, splashing the clear, cool water up to your knees, up to your waist. How inviting that water is, how clean and temperate—not too warm, not too cold—how clean, how translucent with sunlight shining through! How can you resist it? You don't. Suddenly, you leave the shore and run into the water. You plunge into it; you swim and jump and dance in the multi-colored water. You go all the way to the bottom—come up to take a big breath—then again you go to the bottom where you pick up a little shell. Feel the shell; look at it—and let it drop again. Now, you are swimming toward the open sea—fast, at first, like a triumphant champion—then with a slower rhythm. After a while, you turn on your back and rest. Let the water keep you afloat with its resilience—with its strength. You let go of the muscles you have used so well. Just lie on the water as though on your bed. Close your eyes and feel the sustaining energy of the water and the sun. You are floating in liquid energy—in freedom and comfort—while the waves, little by little, bring you back to shore. You step out of the water, contented and relaxed, your mind and body resplendent. You walk to a semishad-owed, quiet place—lie down and enjoy the darkness after the light of the sun—lying there happy and harmonious—the rhythm of the waves joining the rhythm of your breathing in deep union as sleep envelops you.

You may prefer some other forms of activity—skiing in your favorite mountains, bicycling, hiking, or whatever you like.

Choose Your Dream

Put yourself to sleep as you would put a child to sleep; no brutal, violent TV shows, no quarrels or scolding or un-finished business at bedtime. There are sound psychological reasons for the warm quiet communion at bedtime, the gentle story, the soothing lullaby. One may say to oneself, as to a loved child: "What is the worst thing that happened to you today?" And let the child tell what it was, from beginning to end, without interruption or comment, criticism or praise: it happened—let it be. One might say, as to a child, "What would you like to dream tonight?" Again, listen without comment, and say at last, "Yes, now you can go to sleep and dream that dream." It is one of the best preludes to sleep not only for children but also for adults.

With a child this should not become a fixed routine without which he is unable to go to sleep; it is one of many ways to wish good night to children. In any case, one should never allow a child to go to sleep in an upset mood. As we have said, at the time near sleep the division between conscious and subconscious is very tenuous. We do not want a painful emotion to pass this thin barrier and become strongly fixed in the deep mind. This is as true for yourself as for a child.

Warm Magic

This is a preparation of a different order, almost wholly physical and in some ways magical. It was originated by the famous healer and hydrotherapist Father Sebastin Kneipp, who by using water in varied and ingenious ways brought his patients back to health. I have tried this unusual, sleep-inviting method, and so have many of my friends. I know of nothing quite comparable to it.

Make everything ready for the night: windows, lights and extra warm blankets on the bed. Take a comfortable bath or shower. Then, without drying yourself, put a towel around your neck or put on your nightgown or pajama and run quickly, wet as you are, to bed. Switch off your light as you go because, once you are in bed, it is very important to cover yourself completely: pull the blankets tightly around your neck, wrap yourself as in a cocoon, close and tight, with no air between your skin and the covers.

Won't the bed be wet and uncomfortable? you ask. Won't I catch cold?

Not at all. Both you and the bed will be dry in a very short time, although, in all probability, you will be asleep before that happens. The feeling coming from this is extraordinarily deep and soft and warm.

Physiologically, there is no great mystery about this method. We sleep when we are warm, and the circulation rises quickly to the skin to warm and dry it when it is wet.

As a variation to this method, wet a small towel with lukewarm water and wring it out thoroughly. Then, lying in bed, put it over your solar plexus and abdomen, and cover it with a thicker towel, or with a woolen scarf, big enough to wrap around your body. This will draw away any congestion from your head, and a soothing feeling of peacefulness will envelope you.

Another variation is to take your bath or shower wearing a very thin, drip-dry nightgown or pajama. As you come out of the bath squeeze out all the excess water, then put on a thick, warm dressing gown, jump into bed and wrap up tight in your many warm blankets. You will be asleep before your gown or pajama is dry.

Play It Backwards

One of the most effective preludes to "high" quality sleep is also a splendid discipline for the mind.

Pass in review the events of your day, but backwards!

Begin with the last thing you did, just before going to bed; and, with great attention to detail, work back through everything that happened, everything you saw and heard, said and did, every scene, every sensation until you come to the moment when you awoke in the morning. Probably you will be asleep long before you reach your awakening. Looking at our actions in reverse can be highly valuable and balancing. At times the effect is humorous, a little like one of the old film comedies which you have seen in revivals—a little man is run over by a steam roller, knocked down and rolled out quite flat, and then the steam roller rolls backward and up comes the little man, briskly puffing on a cigarette butt.

For instance, suppose this happened to you today: you glanced at your clock and suddenly realized that you were going to be late for an important appointment. Your whole tempo changed—you had to rush to get ready. And everything of course conspired to defeat you—missing buttons, exasperating drivers. You arrived breathless and apologetic—only to discover that you were early—that your clock was fast. Reviewing the experience backwards, knowing the end of the story, you can laugh at all your monumental frustration.

This mental exercise develops both our sense of objectivity and our memory. It is good for us even if it keeps us awake for a few minutes; usually, however, it does not. Most of us fall asleep long before reaching the moment of awakening in the morning.

DO IT! You will be amazed.

Lake Inmost

Unless it is uncomfortable for you, lie on your back with legs and arms spread apart.

Now imagine that:

Your mind is a great, smooth lake high in the mountains. This is Lake Inmost. Now in Lake Inmost you throw a few colored pebbles. These pebbles have a name. Here is a blue one called "lovely." Keep the pebble in your hand for a few moments—feel its texture and weight, see its color and design. Then throw your "lovely" stone into Lake Inmost. In the silence listen to the sound of the stone as it touches the water. Watch the ripples in the water as the circles are getting larger and larger and larger. Then lazily and quietly, as you feel sleep taking over, pick up another colored pebble. Feel it. See it. What would you like to call this? "Strong?" "Happy?" "Good?" "Healthy?" "Quiet?" "Sleep?" Give to your precious stones any name with a good connotation. Throw them slowly and lazily into Lake Inmost. Look at the larger and larger circles that each pebble makes in that water while *you* gently float into beautiful sleep.

Two One, Two One

This is a Yoga method to induce tranquillity.

Count your breathing in this way: One when exhaling —two when inhaling. One—exhaling. Two—inhaling. Nothing more. The art is to do it completely, thinking of nothing else, feeling nothing else, only breathing deeply, fully, out (one) and in (two).

I often use this gentle way to slip into sleep. Instead of directing or counting my breathing, I only observe it—

and go with it. Just follow your breathing. Let it *be*.
Simply follow it. Begin with three or four very complete
breaths. Exhale all the air in the lungs, every last bit of it.
Then, take a full, slow breath through your nose. Fill up
every possible space in your chest. Retain the breath as
long as you can. Now, very, very slowly, exhale it; exhale
all of it. When you think it is all out, there may still be a
little left; let that last little bit out until you are completely
empty. Repeat this three or four times, and then follow
your natural breathing. Keep your attention on that extraordinary act. Just breathing can give a sense of quiet
wonder.

The Numbers Game

A childish but efficacious way of going to sleep is to
count: one, two, three, four. As you count mentally, picture the numbers appearing in succession, white and large
on a black screen. This is a monotonous game, and as you
become increasingly bored the numbers appear more
and more slowly—the screen remains black for longer and
longer intervals . . . the black becomes more and more
velvety . . . more and more soft . . . irresistibly inviting. . . .

A Far Country

Make your whole body as stiff as you possibly can; not
just one part of your body but all of it—stiff, stiff, stiff.
Hold it as long as you can; when it is as stiff as stone and
you think you can hold it no longer, hold it a little
longer—then let go completely.

Repeat this ten times. When you let go for the last
time, project in your mind, as vividly as you can, an image:

it can be your favorite flower; or young animals, kittens or puppies, stretching with lazy grace, then curling up and going to sleep. It can be some peaceful landscape, or anything purely visual and pleasant, anything that is not connected with past or present problems, anything that will take us, slowly and gently, into the far country of sleep.

One more word on this subject: if you are in bed and simply cannot go to sleep, *do not try*. Trying in itself makes you tense. *Trying* includes the possibility of failing. Even if you should succeed in falling asleep, it would probably be, not a restful but a *trying* sleep.

Ask yourself: *how can I use this?* One can make something useful and beautiful even out of a long sleepless night. And it has been thoroughly proven that even staying awake the whole night through has no harmful physiological effects.

Out of a whole night of exploration and study, you may emerge with an important discovery or an answer you have been seeking.

When a night is restless, go with it. *Go with it all the way*. Waiting for you at the end may be tenderness and liberation.

It works—if you work

When we resist part of ourselves, we may become so involved in resisting that we resist unselectively; we resist everything. When you are doing the recipes, resist nothing that comes from your inner self.

29. OPEN THE DOOR TO PLEASURE

> Rengetsu when on pilgrimage came to a village at sunset
> and begged for lodging for the night, but the villagers
> slammed their doors. She had to make a cherry tree in
> the fields her shelter. At midnight she awoke and saw,
> as it were in the spring night sky, the fully opened cherry
> blossoms laughing to the misty moon. Overcome with
> their beauty, she arose and made a reverence toward the
> village:
> "Through their kindness in refusing me lodging,
> I found myself beneath the blossoms on the night of
> the misty moon." *

Few people are as advanced in the art of living as Rengetsu;
even after such complete rejection, she was still open to
pleasure and gratefulness. In similar circumstances, most
of us would have felt bitterness, self-pity, loneliness, a
vengeful resentment against all the world of humanity.

Not Rengetsu. Look at her, immersed in moonlight and
gratitude, bathed in beauty and pleasure, bowing to the
villagers and thanking them for their kindness in refusing
her a night's lodging!

Had Rengetsu been filled with resentment and self-

* *A First Zen Reader*, Trevor Leggett. Tuttle.

pity, her bitter tears would have obscured the beauty of the blossoms and the moon. Had she been able to see the beauty only through the veil of her resentment, she might have responded vengefully, "You selfish villagers, you are punished! God loves *me* and gives to *me* the blossoms and the moon, not to you, wretched creatures shut up in your dark houses."

True pleasure is inextricably linked with feelings of gratitude, generosity, well-being. So inseparable is pleasure from this climate of good feeling that it is hard to know which comes first, the enjoyment or the good feeling.

Yet it is also true that pleasure is often misused as a means of vengeance, an expression of hostility. This is sadistic or masochistic pleasure, a complicated neurotic aberration that requires treatment.

This recipe is not a treatment for the neurotic misuse of pleasure. It is designed to make us aware, open, ready to accept and give pleasure here and now.

Let us put ourselves in the place of Rengetsu. In fact we often are in her place; we do not need to be Oriental mystics in search of a night's lodging to have doors slammed in our faces. How many times has the door of understanding and acceptance been shut against our open or hidden appeal? How many times have *we* slammed our own doors against the appeal of another? And how many times have we thus begun the vicious circle of self-pity and guilt, guilt and self-pity? To stop it we sometimes frantically try to buy pleasure.

This is one of the reasons why the pleasure industry is so prosperous. Witness the convulsive state we are reduced to at Christmas: we rush about in a condition of agitated worry, all the while insisting that we are having a wonderful time. "This is pleasure, pleasure!" we shout, unmindful that doctors and psychotherapists are never so busy as at Christmas time, when half the world is suffering from indigestion, a hangover, or a seasonal neurosis. Perhaps that is why at this season the rate of traffic accidents is so high. Is this pleasure?

There is a vast gulf between this self-conscious and determined pursuit of pleasure and the state of being which perceives, invites, and accepts pleasure. No commercial pleasure industry can produce "the blossoms on the night of the misty moon." Only the inner industry of the mind can create that state of being which is open to pleasure.

To define pleasure is not easy; it is different for each of us. I have asked many people of different temperaments to tell me, not what they have experienced as a particular pleasure, but how they would describe the *state of pleasure*, the experience of pleasure in itself.

The replies had a surprising similarity:

"When I am all one, all together—not a piece of me going one way, another piece going another way, a third reasoning about all these different ways; when I don't discuss or think about pleasure; when pleasure and I are one."

"When I don't even realize that I am in a state of pleasure."

"When I am conscious of the feeling rather than of myself."

"When there is no let-down of any kind, mental or physical."

"When I am not self-centered."

"When pleasure leaves me a better person than I was before."

The state of pleasure is evoked in different ways for each of us. It can come by way of the senses, or from a feeling of accomplishment or through the wish and fulfillment of love. For some the purest, most intense pleasure comes out of close contact with nature; others have known it at the moment of a discovery or insight into themselves. People say, trying to articulate this feeling of inner harmony, "I am myself; I don't stand in my own way."

Often it is the act of making others happy or of creating something beautiful that gives pleasure. When we are very well and aware of our well-being, we feel the pleasure of merely being, of simply moving a hand, of breathing, of opening and shutting the eyes, of feeling the life flowing through us—the pleasure of waking during the night and listening to silence.

When we think of one experience of pleasure in the past, another often comes spontaneously to mind. Ask a friend to tell you about a moment of great pleasure, and see how that friend's mood improves. It is possible to induce deep, therapeutic relaxation merely by reliving past experiences of pleasure. Pleasure that harms no one is good for the body and the spirit.

However, it sometimes happens that, when we think of past pleasure, a sudden, piercing sadness invades us. Those pleasures are gone, gone forever, and there is the wish to cry—then cry—for those tears are better outside of you than inside. They may be gentle tears of nostalgia, or they may be tears of bitterness. Unshed, such tears are often the very thing that makes it hard for you to experience pleasure *now*.

When we are ready in both body and mind to receive pleasure, it comes to us in unexpected ways. This happened to me not long ago. My husband and I, waiting for a connecting flight in a little airport in New Mexico, were sitting in the coffee shop. At the next table to us was a family: father, mother, three boys and a small girl. I felt an impression of harmony in the group, of solidarity and seriousness without strain, of affection so pervasive that it needed no outward expression. The one that impressed me most was the little girl. She was probably not quite three years old, with a strong, healthy face, rosy cheeks, red lips. Her eyes were dark and immensely open, and now they were looking at me. We were looking at each other so completely that my husband's voice seemed far away.

"That child is fascinated by you," he said.

"I am fascinated by her," I answered.

Our mutual absorption was interrupted by the arrival of food. Everyone ate quietly. The time came for the family to leave. The father and three boys started out, the mother followed. But the little girl turned and walked toward our table, looking at me in her intense complete way.

I can see her now. She comes close and we gaze at each other in complete fascination. She is standing in front of me—small, strong, whole. Without moving my lips, wishing only to focus my thoughts and feelings, I murmur, "You are good and beautiful."

No one could have heard me. But the little, open creature received my feeling.

"You too," she said in exactly the same inaudible tone as mine.

Then came a total, wonderful silence; I do not know how long it lasted. I became aware of the mother, standing to one side, quietly waiting. What a wonderful mother! She did not interrupt the good moment; she did not make any meaningless talk; she watched her child, and without disturbing the moment of peaceful intensity she made me aware that it was time I let the child go. I took the little girl's hand, and in a different tone I said, "Goodbye. Now you are going to have a wonderful trip."

Quickly and gaily she said, "Yes!" turned on her heel, and they were gone.

This brief, complete, happy encounter was for me a moment of pleasure. Unexpected, unplanned, unique—it was given to me. Yet if I had not been open to it, I could not have experienced it.

How often does pleasure pass us by because we are not ready to accept it! When we are preoccupied or in pain it is hard even to see, let alone pluck, the flowers of pleasure on our way. We may even walk blindly over them.

Once in Mexico a man came to me to discuss a problem which was keeping him awake at night. I proposed we take a walk. As we went out, I remarked how beautiful the trees and flowers were in the morning sunlight. He quickly agreed without looking, and began at once to speak of his painful situation. The entire gamut of emotions poured from him, all the feelings that he had to repress and disguise in his daily life. He was free enough to jettison much of this accumulated ballast of painful feeling in strong words and tears.

We walked for the best part of an hour. Then the man suddenly stopped and gazed around him. Overcome, he exclaimed, "Look, look—the trees and the hills—how beautiful they are! Never in my life have I seen anything so beautiful!" He repeatedly urged me to look, making certain that I saw what he saw, that I missed no detail of the scene. Finally, unable to express his pleasure in words, he burst into song.

We were standing at exactly the same spot where I had called his attention to the view an hour earlier.

The state of pleasure can be blocked by real impediments such as a gnawing pain, a necessary task to be done whether we like it or not, or external conditions of temperature, noise, smell, and so forth. Life interposes quite enough of these actual obstacles between us and pleasure.

However there are other impediments, which may seem quite as real to us, but which it is definitely within our power to remove. I am speaking of those ghosts of the past which hover about us, invisible yet powerful. These ghosts may be connected with words, with the training and experiences of our childhood, with the memory of someone we loved who is gone.

This recipe has three purposes: to make certain that no ghosts of the past are troubling us, to de-energize and dissolve them if there should be any, and finally to produce in ourselves that state of being in which we invite, accept, and give pleasure.

First let us agree on what pleasure is and is not. Here is a list, to which you may want to add:

Pleasure is anything that:	*Pleasure is* NOT *anything that:*
Hurts no one	Hurts myself
Makes me feel one and undivided	Hurts other people
	Makes me feel divided
Gives me strength and kindness	Is followed by depressed feelings

Brings a sense of new-ness and uniqueness	Is a repetition of a pattern or tends to become an addiction
Gives me a feeling of freedom and light-ness	Gives me a feeling of guilt and opacity

Now here are two groups of questions. Answer them quickly, yes or no. *Do not* use the directions for answering questions given in the recipe "Questions and How to Ask Them." To the following questions just give the first answer that comes to your mind:

First group of questions   *Answers*

Must punishment follow pleasure?

Must my pleasure bring pain to someone else?

Do I diminish pleasure by the fear of losing it?

Or by jealousy?

Possessiveness?

Greediness?

Do I interfere with other people's pleasure?

Do I consider pleasure a forbidden fruit?

Does pleasure interfere with my principles?

Do I feel guilty when I feel pleasure?

Do I think pleasure is connected with sin?

Second group of questions

Is my body-mind open to pleasure?

Do I feel I deserve pleasure?

Am I nicer to people after I have experienced pleasure?

Do I enjoy giving and receiving pleasure?

Do I feel pleasure is good for me?

And for others?

Have you answered the questions? If you have merely read them through, stop now for a moment; go back and answer them, before reading any further. Jot down the answers quickly, no or yes, as you go.

Now: if you answered *no* to all the questions of the first group and *yes* to all those in the second group, good! Go on and enjoy yourself. You have little need of this recipe, but try it for pleasure!

If you answered *yes* to any of the first group, or *no* to any of the second group, there are probably some impediments to your acceptance of pleasure as we defined it earlier.

Pleasure is one of the essential elements of complete living. The aim of the recipes in this book is to get rid of the obstacles to complete living. Any obstacle to your capacity for pleasure stands between you and completeness.

To eliminate your particular impediments, read through these recipes:

"To Hell with Caution"

"Bubble Freedom"

"As If For the First time"

"Love Yourself as You Love Your Neighbor'

"Your Imagination is Yours"

"Throw Words Away"

"Dance Naked with Music"

Among these recipes there are several that apply specifically to questions to which you answered *yes* in the first group or *no* in the second. As you do the recipes, you will discover for yourself which ones can best help you to get rid of obstacles which stand between you and pleasure.

When the inner obstacles are gone, there will be very little need to cultivate pleasure consciously, for you will find it in your surroundings and in your own being. You will look at things that have always been there—clouds, for instance, or the light shining from a window at night, or any familiar detail in your life—and you will take pleasure in them. You may discover with pleasure how bread, simple bread, can taste. The pleasure of having a body will astonish you with its newness.

Helen Keller, who to all appearance was born with less possibility for pleasure than any of us, wrote this:

"In order to attain his highest education the child must be persistently encouraged to extract joy and constructive interest from sight, hearing, touch, smell, and taste. . . . If a mother puts as much gentle art into this delicate fostering of all his physical powers as she does into the task of preserving his health . . . not only will he reach a well-ordered stewardship of his senses, he will also have the best chance of spiritual maturity. . . . Every person, every group thus excellently equipped for living, is the greatest possible contribution to humanity." *

"The best chance of spiritual maturity," "a well-ordered stewardship of the senses." This is profound and compassionate advice for all of us, children and grownups alike.

Here is a way to put that advice into practice:

* "The World Through Three Senses," Helen Keller. *Ladies' Home Journal,* March 1951.

Several times a day, just for an instant or two—stop—
and with full awareness, see, hear, touch, smell, taste,
feel: wherever you are, find one thing within you or outside of yourself, one thing—no matter how hidden or
insignificant or non-existent to anyone else—find one
thing that pleases you.

Now that you have come to the end of this recipe, read
again the opening paragraph. Decide whether to follow my
directions or, by a lightning interior change, follow the
way of Rengetsu. Her gentle story shows the grace that
dwells in the human mind—in her mind, and in ours. For
no matter how many doors life slams in our face, it is
possible to keep open the door to pleasure, and passing
through, initiate the chain reaction of kindness, generosity,
and beauty.

It works—if you work

Put aside, while you are doing the recipes, any notion of better or worse, higher or lower. Put aside comparison, disapproval, justification. Stop judging. Simply do and feel. Let be. Be. Not right and wrong—only cause and effect. Not what ought to be—only what is.

30. PRAJNA NOW

Prajna—to most of us the word is probably a total stranger. That is why I chose it.

There are circumstances in which a word without familiar overtones and associations is preferable to any other.

Prajna is a Sanskrit term, meaning "an ever-present state of grace." This state of grace is not something to be achieved by laborious effort. It is something to be accepted and realized.

It is our personality, our ego, the image that we have of ourselves that shuts us off from the state of grace. In other words, we stand in our own light. How do we get out of our own light?

There are doubtless as many ways as there are human beings. Most of these ways, however, have one element in common: self-knowledge. Sometimes, as in "You Are Not the Target," the approach to self-knowledge and self-transcendence is from the physical side of the mind-body combination. At other times—and this is the case in the present recipe—it is from the mental side that we make our approach. Each of these approaches is effective; it is good to alternate "Prajna Now" with "Target," and "Target" with "Prajna Now."

When we are in mental or physical pain, we find it hard to remember that it is a passing state. We find it hard to realize that, parallel with the immediate state of misery, there is a state exactly opposite to it.

One may or may not believe that this is so. For some of us it may not be easy to accept. However, to assume that it is so will harm no one, especially not one who is in pain.

We suffer—and the more we identify ourselves with suffering the more we suffer. We habitually say: *"I am* sick." *"I have* a pain." "This makes *me* sad." *"I have* one of *my* headaches."

To the sufferer, suffering is an overwhelming fact. Nobody in his right mind can deny its reality. But we do not have to identify ourselves with suffering. *"I* am not identical with this influenza." *"I* am not this headache." "This anger is not I." "This black despair is not I."

Recognition of this fact brings with it a measure of relief. But how can I achieve this recognition? By remembering at the very moment of sickness, irritation, disgust, pain, that I am *not* the sickness, or any of the other states. Not only does this recollection bring a great relief; it also opens our mind to the thought, the idea, of *Prajna* existing *even here and now.*

The next step of this recipe is to give actual direction to our thought through a semantic device, through a conscious and intelligent use of words.

Misused words can do endless harm. (Hence the recipes, "Song Without Words," "TLA-TLA-TLA," "Throw

Words Away," "Don't Throw Words Around.") But words well used can be enormously helpful. Instead of saying, "I have a pain" or "I am confused" or "I am irritated" say, "At this time there is pain." "There is confusion." "There is irritation."

This simple device often works magic. It does so by breaking our identification with the suffering. We recognize a self apart from the pain; we put the pain at arm's length—and already the suffering is lessened. The suffering is manageable, because *now* there is a self separate and apart from the suffering.

In the final step of this recipe words are used to prepare the way for wordlessness, for something which is not to be talked about but lived through and directly experienced. "Prajna NOW."

Let the word be a signal to stop endless soliloquizing, to refrain from inner argument and discussion.

"Prajna NOW."

"Prajna NOW"—But is Prajna a reality? Do we know what the word means?

Stop asking questions. Be open. Be receptive. "Prajna NOW."

Let those two words stand for all that you can remember or imagine, all that it is possible for you to know and feel of a state of wordless bliss, of supreme well being.

"Prajna NOW." Now, at this moment.

"Prajna NOW."

This recipe is in three steps.

We begin by recognizing the undesirable state of affairs.

We then break the ties of habit which connect this undesirable state with the self.

And finally we open ourselves to the experience of liberation.

Thus:

"*I am in pain*" (Or *irritated, tired, sick*)

"*There is a pain.*" (Or *irritation, fatigue, sickness*)

"*Prajna NOW.*"

The study of this recipe may take a little time and thought; but once studied and understood, it can be put to use in a matter of seconds.

With practice the three steps follow one another more and more quickly, until they become all but simultaneous, an act of mind that takes place with the lightning speed of thought.

It may be difficult to believe that such a simple act of mind can change your state of being. No recounting of it will convince you; only practice will. And it is a most interesting practice and a most independent one. For you can practice this in the privacy of your mind in the midst of a crowd. One—two—three: by the act of taking over the direction of your attention, your attitude is changed; your state of being is changed; you yourself are changed.

Carry the title of this recipe in your mind; carry it written down in your pocket or purse. It will remind you that even while you are in the midst of unpleasantness and pain, even though you may be the target of them, you yourself are *not* unpleasantness and pain.

Suppose you are in the dentist's chair and the drill is boring into one of your molars. The chances are that you are identifying yourself with the pain and so reinforcing it, giving it more power over you. But in reality you are *not* this pain. However, the pain cannot be denied. "There is pain." But you do not choose to strengthen this pain by transfusing into it all the energies of your self.

"There is pain." There is also Prajna.

"Prajna NOW."

Or another example. You are in the midst of a heated business conference. Suddenly your mind becomes cloudy, your thinking ceases to be clear.

Then stop for three or four seconds. Recognize what is happening. You may be thinking, "I am confused."

Do not identify. Simply recognize the fact. The fact is: "There is confusion."

But confusion is not I and I am not it. And remember that, as well as passing confusion there is also Prajna. "Prajna NOW." Prajna at every moment, whenever you choose to open the door and allow yourself to be aware of it. "Prajna NOW."

Then take a deep breath and continue the discussion. Nobody will have noticed that you were doing anything out of the ordinary. The only noticeable fact will be that your thinking has become clearer.

"Prajna NOW."

It works—if you work

Through experiencing the recipes you will become able to be yourself completely, then to put yourself aside and "jump into the other's place." This ability brings freedom and compassion. Enhance it by using it.

31. INVENT ANOTHER

In the first lines of this book we talked of three elementary discoveries.

Discovery number one: Each one of us has, in varying degree, the power to make himself and others feel better or worse.

Discovery number two: Making others feel better is much more fun than making them feel worse.

Discovery number three: Making *others* feel better generally makes *us* feel better.

This is true of everyone, even of one who thinks himself as of no importance, no consequence at all. After an attentive, honest examination, this person will realize that every day, often many times a day, he can choose to be a giver of pain or of pleasure. Regardless of individual differences we all have this built-in ability; practicing the recipes will make you more and more aware of it. You will also notice how this ability increases by using it. You will realize more and more how important you are as a contributor to the sum total of suffering or happiness.

Another point has been emphasized in this book: that

each one of us has a fund of creative potential—either we use it creatively or it will boomerang destructively upon ourselves and others. With these two points in mind, what should the directions for the last recipe be?

First I suggest that you outline for yourself a program to practice the recipes and be able to use them whenever needed. The tempo of living varies widely from person to person. Generally speaking, however, it seems to me that it is possible to become quite proficient in two or possibly three recipes a month. The goal is to have a repertory of recipes to serve you in a very great number of circumstances of living. These recipes are to become your tools, ready and handy at any time. Only practice and familiarity with them will accomplish this.

The other direction of this recipe is one I hope everyone will welcome. It is:

Invent another

You may invent a recipe that suits your situation precisely, one that is made to order for you. Or the recipe you invent may be effective not only for you but also for others. In either case you will use creatively your creative potential. You will enhance your own and other people's well-being.

With a collection of original recipes from persons of different temperaments, constitutions, nationalities, creeds, races, we would have a:

WORLD ENCYCLOPEDIA OF RECIPES FOR LIVING AND LOVING.

In this way you would become an active, radiant link in a chain reaction of the kind that we all most urgently need.

Never before in the history of humanity has the delicate

balance between the forces of destruction and creation
been so perilously poised. We cannot afford to lose even
the smallest opportunity to tip the balance in favor of intelligence, beauty, and love.

APPENDIX

Table of Personal Relationships

People I must deal with but who make me nervous

You Are Not the Target
Prajna NOW
How Can I Use This?
The Tether Ball
Be an Animal
Jump Into the Other's Place
Bubble Freedom
Air, Water, Food

People I feel are trying to control me

Attend Your Funeral
Questions and How to Ask Them
TLA-TLA-TLA
Emergency!
To Hell With Caution
Jump Into the Other's Place
Lay the Ghost
Dance Naked with Music

People I believe I like but who upset me

Bubble Freedom
Ice Cubes in a Flowing River
To Hell With Caution
TLA-TLA-TLA
Air, Water, Food
Questions and How to Ask Them
Open the Door to Pleasure
Prajna NOW

People I wish to or do control

Attend Your Funeral
Go With It
Jump Into the Other's Place
Don't Throw Words Around

People I do not know, but I would like to know

To Hell With Caution
Help Me for I Envy You
How Can I Use This?
Jump Into the Other's Place

People whom I suspect of not liking me, and who seem to pick on me

You Are Not the Target
Jump Into the Other's Place
The Tether Ball
Ice Cubes in a Flowing River
Throw Words Away

Questions and How to Ask Them
Love Yourself as You Love Your Neighbor
Are You Cultivating Today Your Neurosis of Tomorrow?
Open the Door to Pleasure

People I wish would like me

Dance Naked with Music
Give Something for Nothing
Jump Into the Other's Place
TLA-TLA-TLA
Open the Door to Pleasure

People I fear

Questions and How to Ask Them
Ice Cubes In a Flowing River
The Tether Ball
Lay the Ghost
Help Me for I Envy You
The Art of Converting Energy
Bubble Freedom
Throw Words Away
Love Yourself as You Love Your Neighbor

People I irritate, purposely or not

To Hell With Caution
Your Imagination is Yours
Jump Into the Other's Place
Bubble Freedom
Dance Naked with Music
TLA-TLA-TLA
Air, Water, Food

People who bore me

> You Are Not the Target
> How Can I Use This?
> Invent Another
> Go With It
> Open the Door to Pleasure
> Bubble Freedom
> The Art of Converting Energy

People I believe I love completely

Check your love with what St. Paul has to say about love. Here is a list, according to him, of what love is—or is not.*

> Love is patient and kind.
> Love is not jealous or boastful.
> Love is not arrogant or rude.
> Love does not insist on its own way.
> It is not irritable or resentful.
> It does not rejoice in the wrong; but rejoices
> in the right.
> Love:
>> Bears all things.
>> Believes all things.
>> Hopes all things.
>> Endures all things.

* From a suggestion of the Indian lecturer Aly Wassil.

INDEX:

Which Recipes for What Needs?

Go With It
Invent Another
Bubble Freedom
As If for the First Time
Open the Door to Pleasure
To Hell With Caution
Emergency!

CHILDREN

Air, Water, Food
Be an Animal
Throw Words Away
Don't Throw Words Around
Tender is the Night
The Tether Ball
Jump Into the Other's Place
Questions and How to Ask
 Them

COMPLEXION, improvement of:

Air, Water, Food
Bubble Freedom
 See also: BEAUTY, improve-
 ment of

DEPRESSION

How Can I Use This?
Air, Water, Food
Questions and How to Ask
 Them
You Are Not the Target
Ice Cubes in a Flowing River
Dance Naked With Music
Are you Cultivating Today
 your Neurosis of Tomorrow?

Your Imagination is Yours
The Art of Converting En-
ergy

DIGESTION, improvement of:

Air, Water, Food
Throw Words Away
You Are Not the Target
Dance Naked With Music
Emergency!
Be an Animal
 See also: SLEEPLESSNESS,
 TENSION

DISCONTENT

Questions and How to Ask
 Them
Love Yourself as You Love
 Your Neighbor
How Can I Use This?
Go With It
Attend Your Funeral
Invent Another
To Hell With Caution
 See also: BOREDOM

EMOTIONS—See Table of
Personal Relationships

ENERGY

Air, Water, Food
Be an Animal
Lay the Ghost
The Art of Converting Energy
Bubble Freedom
The Tether Ball

WISDOM

The purpose of all the Recipes is to increase practical wisdom, which in the context of this book may be defined as the harmony of instinct, intelligence and love.